S·H·A·R·P-
D·R·E·S·S·E·D
M E N

S·H·A·R·P-
D·R·E·S·S·E·D
M·E·N

BEHIND THE SCENES
FROM BLUES TO BOOGIE
TO BEARDS

David Blayney

NEW YORK

David Blayney has retired from the rock and roll "bidness" and is currently living an abnormally normal life posing as a Stepford Husband in Houston, Texas.

Designed by Casey Choron, March Tenth, Inc.

Library of Congress Cataloging-in-Publication Data

Blayney, David.
Sharp dressed men : ZZ Top behind the scenes from blues to boogie to beards / David Blayney.—1st ed.
p. cm.
ISBN 0-7868-8005-8
1. ZZ Top (Musical group) 2. Rock musicians—United States—Biography. I. Title.
ML421.Z98B6 1994
782.42166′092′2—dc20   93-42412
[B]   CIP
                             MN

FIRST EDITION

10 9 8 7 6 5 4 3 2 1

For Daria,
the love and light of my life,
without whom this would
not have been plausible.

ACKNOWLEDGMENTS

To Mike Duran and Pat Coleman, of Southern Literary, for saddling up a longshot and whipping it all the way to the starting gate.

To Ruth Gray for piloting her trusty laser jet through murky air.

To Chris Pezman for showing me the program.

To Jeff and Elizabeth Martin (the "Trackmaster" and "Diskmistress") for lending their machine and providing a break in the routine.

To Linden Hudson and Dan Mitchell for giving their perspectives.

And to all those whose negative reinforcement gave me the positive resistance to undercome my passive attack.

CONTENTS

PART III
RUNNIN' HARD

PART IV
RUNNIN' ON

FOREWORD

All I can say about what's written in this book is that it is the truth. I watched it happen.

Between 1969 and 1984 I served as ZZ Top's lighting director, lighting designer, production manager, production designer, stage manager, and general overall galley slave, either all at once or in some combination of the aforementioned roles. I did just about everything there was to do except book the shows, play the music, and collect the money.

My acquaintance with the band's members goes back to before the formation of ZZ Top. I went to high school in Houston with Billy Gibbons in the days when he was just another kid who played guitar. I met Dusty Hill and Frank Beard a little bit later, in their days as part of the Dallas band called the American Blues. After things got going with ZZ Top, I lived with Frank or Dusty off and on for several years, and the three of us became a close-knit bunch of friends. All of which is to say that if a book can be written about how ZZ Top started, matured, then grew into an international music attraction, my experiences put me in a logical position to be the storyteller.

What follows is a roughly historical assemblage of tales and recollections. Details of incidents that I didn't personally witness or partake in, I heard straight from the mouths of those who did. A lot of these stories are humorous. Some critics may accuse me of a "positive stream of consciousness" approach because of this. Let 'em. To me, it's just the way things came down. Here and there, to help the flow of the narrative, I have taken the liberty of using both dialogue and dialect as I thought they were needed. These are intended only to convey the sense of the experience, not absolute historical reality. Wherever I needed to step an inch into speculation, I have admitted it on the spot.

In a book like this, the writer's own life as a "participant observer" tends to become inextricable from the broader account being attempted. I have not resisted this tendency, and for a good reason. In addition to telling the story of ZZ Top, I wanted to do something else which, as far as I know, hasn't yet been done in depth. I wanted to convey what it was like to be one of the support troops behind a rock and roll band, one of the largely unseen, unknown people who are there behind the scenes creating and then presenting all the sights and sounds that audiences have come to expect from a stage band. In this particular case the band and the crew happened to be from Texas, but the pattern was approximately the same for all the other groups, large and small, who were around at the time.

I hope you enjoy reading this book as much as I enjoyed writing it. It was not something I thought about doing while I was on the road with the Boys for all those years. It just started to happen one night when I had a few quiet moments alone, and gradually grew into something I wanted to do for myself. As to its greater value, you will have to be the judge of whether or not I have succeeded as both historian and eyewitness-sociologist, and, hopefully, as an entertainer in my own right.

DAVE BLAYNEY
Houston, Texas

PART I

RUNNIN' LEAN

1

FROM DELTA BLUES
TO TEXAS BOOGIE

Z Top has been around a long time now—long enough for the Boys to gain some prestige, lose a little hair, and move into the ranks of rock and roll's most respected elder statesmen. Some of their songs, like "La Grange," are so widely known that they instantly call up an image of wild cars, desert landscapes, and the Texas boogie power trio itself, the Smith Brothers of Rock. Billy Gibbons, Dusty Hill, and Frank Beard: the band with the midnight shades, the Father Time beards, and the piledriver counterpoint. To many lovers of rock, it's like they have always been there.

But naturally there was a beginning.

Most bands form, play together a few years, then break apart and vanish. Their members may momentarily (or longer) resurface in other groups and become famous or perpetuate fame they have already established; more likely they just drop out of sight altogether, disappearing into the non-musical mainstream. Some of them become has-beens who never were and wind up dying a lingering musical death in the pale spotlight of a seedy lounge in a cheap motel. The old "Weren't-you-almost-famous-once?" routine. Only truly major bands manage to survive the many hazards of the music business long enough to grab hold of a permanent place in it for themselves.

ZZ Top is one of the fortunate few to get to the top and stay there. Why was this?

A successful band is usually made up of more than just skilled musicians. As is said in the Southern part of the industry, "Talent don't mean dick." A player needs more than just above-average musical skill to attain success in the industry. He also needs someone to direct and nurture his skills and talents, and perhaps even discover and develop qualities that were previously lying dormant. A mediocre musician could stumble upon an intelligent and tenacious manager and wind up being a superstar. Conversely, a musical genius could hook up with an inept manager and never move past performing in the Bubbles 'n Troubles Lounge. This has happened to potential stars who signed on with guys who couldn't manage a two-hole outhouse in an Ex-Lax factory. A delicate and often elusive chemical balance between artist and manager is usually a prerequisite for success.

ZZ Top has lasted all these years because it combines a lucky mix of above-average technical ability, musical inspiration, studio savvy, and on-stage spontaneity. There's also been a great deal of highly competent behind-the-scenes managerial energy and direction involved, too. The interplay between the two factors eventually blended into an intangible harmony. In other words, ZZ Top is a band loaded with skills *and* brains.

Add to this the fact that ZZ Top launched a distinct subspecies of American rock and roll and remains its number one purveyor. Texas boogie has Southern blues roots amplified into a hard-driving, heavily rhythmic sound never before attempted in quite the same way. The band and its music have matured over time without losing the full-tilt boogie power that makes it so distinctive.

For those of you who are either too young to remember or were too stoned to notice at the time, let me take a moment to mention where Texas Boogie fit into the musical swirl that was boiling up when ZZ Top was born in 1969.

After World War II, the big band sound that had dominated popular music for a generation began to falter under the rising double whammy of two music styles. One would eventually be named rock and roll, and the other was the blues. Elvis Presley, the white boy who could sing like a black man, came out of Memphis in 1954 and shook and shimmied the music business to its roots. On his heels from elsewhere in the South were Roy Orbison, Jerry Lee Lewis, and Buddy Holly, all mixing traditional Southern patterns of black music directly into the musical setting opened up by electric instrumentation. The main influence on this new music seems to have been the blues as played in the New Orleans–Memphis axis, the Delta of the Mississippi Valley.

Amplifiers made it possible for small, intense bands to form in which a lead guitarist, bass, and drums were integral parts, sometimes joined by a rhythm guitar and/or keyboardist. Some or all of the band members sang at the same time they were playing. This particular musical offshoot would later be referred to as rockabilly and would eventually evolve into what became known as Southern rock. These newly electrified groups began to appear everywhere, smaller but with a sound every bit as solid as the old big band orchestras. Maybe economics had something to do with what happened, since operating costs for the little amplified groups were a fraction of what it took for the orchestras to keep going. At some point in the 1950s the importance of the big bands became musical history. The electrified smaller band concept was beginning to spread around the United States, and other regional styles of music—like Motown—began to evolve.

It is never really possible to figure why one subspecies of musical innovation moves up faster than another, but in the case

5

of Southern rock (or rockabilly) there is little doubt that Elvis's two years in the Army—Jerry Lee Lewis's public relations problem stemming from ill-advisedly marrying his thirteen-year-old cousin—and Buddy Holly's death in a small plane crash had something to do with the change of music's inertial drive which occurred in the early 1960s. Beginning roughly with the American tour of the Beatles in 1964, America's musical trends were paced by new variants of rock and roll based elsewhere. Leading the charge was the Liverpool sound of the Beatles, accompanied quickly by the louder, brasher offshoots of British music reinvented by the Rolling Stones and the Animals but heavily influenced by the Delta blues. Southern rock didn't go away by any means, but it awaited resurgence at the hands of new musical innovators.

The political turmoil of the middle and late 1960s was accompanied by an important change in rock and roll offerings. From the West Coast, blown in on a cosmic wind of psychedelic philosophy based in the counterculture movement, came the Jefferson Airplane and the Grateful Dead, playing a musical form eventually dubbed acid rock, named presumably in honor of the drug of choice favored by many musicians and fans alike. This music was damned near as scary as its name. It was wild and eerily hypnotic stuff that helped introduce to the American scene the notion of uninhibited experimentation, musical and otherwise. Listeners were lyrically encouraged to take Dr. Timothy Leary's advice and "Turn on, tune in, and drop out." Unfortunately, some of them also dropped dead.

Our entire culture was obviously affected by a simple musical style. Television commercials, once boring and plain vanilla, now seethed with color and images of fantasy. The music developed by bands such as the Airplane and the Grateful Dead inspired all sorts of spinoff retailing—even the manufacture and sale of sheets and pillowcases bursting with stars of the cosmos and dripping rainbows from Oz. Although the comparatively milder music influenced by some British groups was still around, it was bowled over and seemed less important from then on. Also, heavy metal, courtesy of Led Zeppelin, loomed on the horizon.

And now things began to stir down South again. What acid rock offered in intensity, and British rock in style, Southern rock equaled or surpassed in feeling. For this reason, young people who were tired of England's version of bubblegum music, called the Mersey beat, and had used up all of their "E" coupons on the music roller coaster of psychedelia, started to look toward the South and its music, searching for new musical answers to old musical questions. And they found them. There were kids just getting started in Southern rock music who had something to say and they were saying it hot.

All of which history, jammed into a nutshell, brings me to the roots of ZZ Top. Houston, Texas, is where things started in 1969. The reason why I know about it and became involved with the Boys is that Houston is my hometown, too.

Musicians are drawn early to the creation of music, generally before their teens. Playing music is a social thing, so kids get together with their instruments to jam and fool around. If they're talented enough, the next step for a fledgling garage band, as they came to be known, is to line up a tentative gig or two, perhaps at a school dance. Then an irregular pattern of performances will start, lasting through high school or even college. Not a lot of money is involved; the bandsmen play mainly just for the fun of performing. Most of the time these kids grow up and slide into the standard mode of getting married, having a family, making a straight living. The instruments are put aside, only to be dragged out once in a while for parties or perhaps gigs on weekends in local saloons.

Ninety-nine percent of the musicians in this world fit this generalization. For the one-percenters left over, music isn't something that can be put aside. It becomes a consuming passion for which hardships will gladly be endured. This frequently includes earning a miserable income even if "success" is achieved. Most professional musicians, surviving by playing and singing, make a

7

puny yearly income. But to them it just doesn't matter: making the music is enough.

And then there is the tiny percent of these musicians who through luck, wit, and staying power get up on that soundwave and ride. Somtimes an individual musician, no matter how talented, can't get a spotlight in a prison break. But with the right combination of other musicians, things can click almost overnight. In ZZ Top's case, it all began with the love of music held by a kid in my high school who was one in a million. His name was Billy Gibbons.

William Frederick Gibbons, a.k.a. the Reverend Willie G., Worthless Willie, B. G., or just plain Billy, was born in Houston on September 16, 1949, to Fred and Lorraine Gibbons. At first glance Billy has always *seemed* to be a normal person, and in fact he can portray that role if he wants. But inside, all is different. Take him apart and you find a brilliant musician and a zany comedian who is a pathological yarn-spinner. His creative juices are in perpetual motion, whether it has to do with music or just everyday life. He is constantly firing one in from left field like a frozen rope peg to home plate. You never know what he'll come up with next: You just know that it will be plenty different.

Billy's musical genius is inherited from his father, an excellent keyboardist who played professionally around the Houston area from the 1940s to the 1980s. Freddie Gibbons did it all, from providing the organ music between innings at Houston's old Buffalo Stadium to conducting the Houston Symphonic Orchestra. Billy's dad had an ear for pitch so perfect that he could tell when the air conditioner at home was going on the blink because it was changing its sound ever so slightly. When Billy was a kid he used to play a musical game with his dad in which Billy would form the most outlandish guitar chords possible, using all of his fingers in a weird tangle on the fretboard. Freddie, with his back turned, would listen to the chord strummed and not only name it but also tick off the notes played by each string. Having a dad like that was a big inspiration to Billy, as was seeing him play on stage, so it was probably inevitable that he would make a stab at life as a professional musician.

His personal musical direction, however, was guided by the Houston scene of the 1950s and 1960s. Rock and roll was big after Elvis, and young Billy listened to and loved the sounds being created. But he was also strongly influenced by the Gibbons family's maid, Big Stella, and her daughter, Little Stella. They exposed Billy to the blues sounds of Jimmy Reed, Howlin' Wolf, and T-Bone Walker. Since Houston was a hotbed of rhythm and blues clubs, Billy was able to see local blues heroes such as Bobby "Blue" Bland and Lightnin' Hopkins in person. Early on, these musicians' vocal and playing styles became a major passion for him, and the old-time blues patterns would influence all of the music Billy later composed and played.

The first thing I ever remember hearing about Billy Gibbons was that he was the funniest kid in Robert E. Lee High School. He had a high profile as a class clown and wild jokester. When somebody said that Billy was funny, it very definitely held dual connotations. Billy was both funny as in *comedian,* and funny as in *peculiar.* In no time at all he was also known as a musician with a lot of talent.

It is hard to think of Billy Gibbons today without a guitar in his hands, but early on he experimented with straight singing and briefly with drumming. In 1963 Fred and Lorraine gave Billy a Gibson Melody Maker and Fender Champ amplifier, and that was the end of the drums. He finally owned the instrument to which he has since been most drawn.

Billy's first gigging band was called the Coachmen; the first time I heard him play was with this group at a high school dance in 1966. When the Coachmen broke up in 1967, Billy and its drummer, Dan Mitchell, regrouped with two other kids, Don Summers and Tom Moore, to form a new band they named the Moving Sidewalks. The idea behind the Sidewalks was to get in on the psychedelic music sweeping across the country at the time. A song that the Coachmen had originally recorded, "99th

Floor," was recorded again by the Sidewalks and was number one on the radio in Houston for several weeks, a suggestion of things ahead for Billy Gibbons. The Sidewalks were a hot band, and Billy's reputation as a badass guitar player was launched.

If you had a reputation as a guitar slinger in the Houston of the 1960s, all the other young guitar top guns would want to try you out. Quite often groups were booked in a "battle of the bands" event. The Sidewalks once had to do battle with a Dallas band called the Chessmen in which Billy found himself up against a player rumored to be "only sixteen years old." The hot young picker was Jimmy Vaughn, who later became the original guitar player with the Fabulous Thunderbirds and is the older brother of the late Stevie Ray Vaughn. Frank Beard and Dusty Hill told me that they saw the shootout between Gibbons and Vaughn and claim that Jimmy won, but they've always been prejudiced in favor of Dallas bands. Of course, whoever really was the winner that night turned out to be totally unimportant; twenty years later both young guitar slingers wound up as very successful musicians, lethal on lead guitar. Incidentally, the "only sixteen" rumor has stuck with Jimmy down through the years. For all I know he may actually be "only sixteen," with a secret portrait of himself hanging on his wall that makes him look about ninety-two.

As the Sidewalks toured around Texas and Louisiana, they became legendary for the various smoke and eruptions that punctuated their stage shows. Gibbons loved explosions and smoke, so his show just naturally had to have plenty of pyrotechnics. Back in those days city fire marshals weren't called in before a show to check out the explosive charges or, for that matter, the credentials of the kids setting them up. Instead they let anyone with a band do whatever they wanted. Can you imagine a minion of the state turning loose an unsupervised young musician with a keg of black powder these days? But that's the way it worked in the sixties. Whoever felt like mixing the chemicals for the explosive charges just went for it, and the club owner hoped there'd be something left of his place on Sunday morning.

Since things were dog-eat-dog between bands, groups found themselves doing anything to get an edge over their rivals. The prevailing philosophy was simple: Whoever was biggest, loudest, and flashiest was also the bestest. Dan Mitchell was usually the "chemist" with the Sidewalks' charges, out of personal interest and a certain flair for the task. Once his enthusiasm led to an explosion a bit bigger and closer than he anticipated and he almost vaporized the side of his head. The Sidewalks had been opening for Ten Years After that night, and the After's lead guitarist, Alvin Lee (later immortalized in the movie *Woodstock*), helped get Dan to the hospital. Fortunately Dan wasn't seriously injured, but I expect that his hearing was impared for a while.

Billy on some occasions would supervise the loading of the show explosives himself. His thing was SOUND, leading him to argue in favor of doubling all charges to ensure optimum "effect." Thus he courted disaster and made every flashpot cue an adventure. One time Billy succeeded so well at being the biggest and loudest that he also became the hottest. By accident a charge was touched off too close to some tinder-dry stage items, setting them ablaze. The explosion fried some grillcloth, cooked some speakers, and torched a backdrop. The whole club almost went up in smoke and the crowd loved it. Billy was a great showman, always ready to take a risk. No insurance agent in the country would even talk to him, so they said.

Whether it was *because* of or in *spite* of their dubious stage show, the Sidewalks wound up one time on a four-show mini-tour to Houston, Dallas, and San Antonio, opening for guitar legend Jimi Hendrix. Jimi peered through the billows of smoke and explosions and found himself liking the Sidewalks' young lead guitar player. Legend (according to Billy Gibbons) has it that Jimi mentioned Billy on "The Tonight Show" shortly after this series of gigs. When asked who the up-and-coming guitar players were to watch for, Jimi's reply was supposedly, "Billy Gibson of the 'Lectric Sidewalks." People were always confusing his last name like that, and some still do today.

Exactly on which show Jimi said this is unknown, and it may be one of Billy's homespun yarns. The grounds for skepticism come from a question mark associated with a second tale Billy tells about Hendrix. He told me a story about being in the Sidewalks' dressing room an afternoon before one of the Hendrix shows. Since the Sidewalks had a keyboard player, a small electric piano was set up in there. Billy said that he was sitting there alone playing his guitar when he looked up to see Jimi peeking around the door with a smile on his face. "I thought I heard somethin' 'lectric," he said. Jimi then proceeded to sit down and jam with Billy a little, but instead of playing guitar he used the keyboard. Billy claims that in friendship Jimi Hendrix later gave him a pink Stratocaster guitar. On the other hand Billy's friend Kurt Linhof, a local Houston musician, says that he remembers painting that guitar himself in Billy's garage along with two others. The truth lies somewhere in the caverns of Billy's mind.

Jimi Hendrix wasn't the only person whose attention was caught by Billy Gibbons in the late 1960s. The Moving Sidewalks' popularity was due primarily to Billy's virtuosity with his guitar, and something beyond ability suggested that he was destined for bigger and better things. Unfortunately for the rest of the band, Billy's stardom would not be achieved in the vehicle of the Sidewalks. The band faded into psychedelic oblivion in 1969 when keyboardist Tom Moore and bass player Don Summers were both drafted into the Army, mobilized due to the Vietnam conflict.

Just before this happened, Billy was spotted one night by a young record promoter who introduced himself as Bill Ham. He was enthusiastic about Billy's music and said so. "You boys are stronger than forty acres of onions!" was the exact quote, according to Dan Mitchell. Several weeks later, Billy, with his Sidewalks friends on the way to basic training, agreed to let Ham have a shot at managing his career. The young man with the hot guitar and the older man with the knowledge and strategy melded a rare and formidable combination of intuition and skills. If a particular moment can be set for the start of ZZ Top, it was when the contract between Billy Gibbons and Bill Ham was signed.

"Billy Mac" Ham, the pride of Waxahatchie, Texas (just south of Dallas), at that point was working for H. W. Daily's record distributorship in Houston. He had formerly been a singer in the Pat Boone style, but that career had lasted only through the recording of a single, "Dream On," on the Dot record label. Ham was supercharged with ambition, not intending to stick with Daily long. His intensity had already won him a gold 45 record from Creedence Clearwater Revival for the part he had played in making their first record, "99 and 1/2," a success in the Houston area. He was now in the market to become an independent manager of new talent and was especially interested in lining up someone with qualities suitable for molding into a rock and roll superstar— somebody exactly like Billy Gibbons. Ham's background in music, combined with an appreciation of military discipline and regimentation and a certain ruthless determination, made him seem ideal in Billy's mind for the role of directing a new career.

I have to agree with that estimation. When I later got to know him, I realized that Bill Ham was one of the most totally self-confident men to ever come down the road. He always told me, and everybody else around him, that he never wanted to hear the words *can't, no,* or *impossible.* The words were not acceptable even if overwhelming evidence suggested otherwise. Ham coupled a Col. Tom Parker managerial savvy with a Rambo approach to life and a Marquis de Sade style of doing business, which would soon make him famous in the music industry. "If I tell y' a rooster can pull a freight train, boy, you better hitch 'im up," became his motivational rallying cry. Some onlookers in awe (and no little fear of crossing swords with him) likened Bill Ham to a pit bull on methedrine or a human buzz saw.

Billy and Ham wasted no time in putting together a new band with Billy as the nucleus. The new group would not, however, be formed with the intention of playing acid rock. The notion was to start things off with the band's feet planted firmly in the blues but powered up with amplification, a muscular drum beat, and a driving instrumental interplay between the lead and bass guitar players. There was also plenty of opportunity for expansive guitar parts. It was an idea well-suited to Billy's musical tastes: bluesy and loud. Out of this came, as all the world now knows, the creation of Texas Boogie and the enormous success of ZZ Top.

2

"ARTISTS'RE FUNNY, BOY!"

The music business has a lot of off-beat personalities associated with it. Bill Ham would write off the strange behavioral patterns of musicians by shrugging and saying: "Artists're funny, boy!" *Flakey* would also be an acceptable substitute for *funny*. When he and Billy began trying to find the right pieces to fit into their musical puzzle they tried out a varied array of "artists." These came and went like cats over a fence, and when it came time to explain *why* they went, Ham simply invoked his four-word axiom and went on without a second thought.

Billy started ZZ Top with Dan Mitchell (all that was left of the Moving Sidewalks) and a human cartoon of a keyboard-playing friend of his, Lanier Greig. Lanier was a former member of the Houston group called Neil Ford and the Fanatics and began sitting in on keys with the Sidewalks after Tom Moore was drafted. His comic nature and flamboyance were almost a photocopy of Billy's.

From time to time Billy and Lanier would appear around Hermann Park in downtown Houston wearing amazing rigs, such as homemade Mickey Mouse suits with old records for ears, or whiteface clown makeup. They did it for other people's laughs but mostly just for their own. Just to see how far you could go before a puffing team in white coats from the county asylum came charging up with a D-ring jacket and a net to throw over you.

Once Billy, Dan, and Lanier got together, they decided that since the new band was to have a blues direction it was obviously time for a name change. This brings up one of the big questions about ZZ Top. Where in the hell did that name come from? Once I heard Gibbons let it slip that Lanier was its author, but Billy covered up fast and changed the subject. At any rate, all three of the original ZZ Toppers went down to the Harris County Courthouse together one day in 1969 and registered the name.

Over the years I worked for Billy, I asked him on three separate occasions to tell me the *real* truth about the origin of the name. I got three totally different answers. One was that the old trio were looking for a black and bluesy sounding name like B. B. King or Z. Z. Hill. Running through different combinations of initials, ZZ Top "just came up." Another version of the story was that Billy and Lanier were driving down the highway one day and saw a billboard with part of the top advertisement torn off, which in turn exposed some of an older one underneath. Lo and behold! The old and new letters combined in such a fashion as to spell (or at least suggest) ZZ Top. The third and most plausible version Billy offered was that they just combined the names of two popular reefer rolling papers (Zig Zag and Top) and bingo, a legend was born. I bet if I asked Billy again there would be a fourth story. Artists're funny, boy! My money's on version three.

The first ZZ Top incarnation was Billy on guitar, Dan on drums, and Lanier on keyboard, carrying bass on the footpedals of his organ. Thus equipped, in 1969 the three of them went to Robin Hood Brian's studio in Tyler, Texas, and recorded ZZ's first single, "Salt Lick," with Billy dubbing additional bass guitar for the song. I heard this song over my car radio not long afterward and remember noticing the distinctive sound. At that point I didn't know my high school acquaintance, Billy Gibbons, was part of the group; I just knew that I really liked what I was hearing. And a lot of other fans in the Houston area did, too.

ZZ Top's startup combination of personnel wasn't destined to last long, and the only gig worth mentioning was the first one. It took place at a joint in Houston called the Love Street Light Circus and Feelgood Machine. You can surmise from the name that this wasn't exactly a country and western bar. It was one of those late-sixties psychedelic clubs that specialized in hurling multicolored splashes of light on its walls in a wholehearted attempt to melt the minds of all patrons, who would in turn occasionally hurl their own multicolored splashes on the floor in a testimony to the fact that their minds were indeed melted. The company that Love Street hired to put on this light show was called Jelly Wall Eyes Pack, a name that says it all. The place definitely did *not* have an atmosphere conducive to playing the blues.

The three band members had a rented limousine for this debut, the idea being to make a triumphant entrance into the club. Unfortunately the place was located three stories up in an old building on Buffalo Bayou near Allen's Landing. The main access was via an outdoor stairway that wasn't much wider than a fire escape, so there went the triumphant entry. It's hard for a band to maintain its cool after puffing up three flights of stairs. Instead of the spectacle of Cleopatra's entrance into Rome, it must have more closely resembled a group of aging marathon runners wheezing up to the finish line. This was the only time ZZ would play the place; the combination of locale and ambience just didn't cut it. I'm sure the roadies who had to lug all the equipment (including Lanier's organ) up three flights appreciated never hitting *that* particular dive again.

It only took a few weeks for Billy and Dan to realize that although Lanier was fun and a solid keyboard player, he just wasn't working out. The band needed a kickass bass player to provide the bottom end of the bluesy sound Billy was seeking. Maybe Bill Ham played a role in what happened next; he never hesitated when it came to making big decisions, even if somebody's ego got chopped into hamburger. It was decided that Lanier had to go, and go he did. Using the excuse that Lanier had deserted them by going to New York for a few days to audition for an acting part, but not really wanting to hurt his feelings by firing him, Billy and Dan more or less quit the band together. I wonder what Lanier thought when all of a sudden ZZ Top came back to life without him a month or so later! But that's the way it happened. Adios, amigo.

Since Lanier had no copyrights on any material, and since Ham had talked him out of being on the credits of "Salt Lick," Lanier Greig slid quietly out of the ZZ Top picture. Probably due to his friendship with Billy, and the fact that Billy promised to "take care of him" in the future, Lanier didn't even try to retain his one-third of ZZ's name. Twenty years later, Lanier is still waiting to be "taken care of," so far as I know.

Billy and Dan began looking for somebody to fit the ticket on bass. In the flux of musicians around Houston it didn't take long. They found their man in the person of Billy Ethridge, former bass player for the Chessmen, up in Dallas, who was loose and looking around. He was a real pro, and a much stronger musician than Lanier Greig had been. Of course, he had his quirks. He took no shit off nobody and played his ax solid with a quarter instead of a pick. Billy thought this second Billy held up the sort of power bass ZZ Top needed, and Ethridge signed on.

ZZ lasted like this for another short time, but it was soon evident that *Dan* was becoming the odd man out. Happily, Dan's musical interests had already begun to fade by this time. He was starting to enjoy success in a clothing store he had as a sideline in Houston called Mr. Fantasy, after the well-known Traffic song. He had just gotten married. When Dan came to rehearsal one day and found a friend of Ethridge's sitting in extemporaneously on

tion bass players at the same time. In this fashion they filtered through several musicians, but they couldn't seem to find the right combination. Finally Frank talked Billy into giving an "old podnah" of his a tryout. Sound familiar? Just like Ethridge before him, Frank wanted a Dallas bud to help hold down the rhythm section. It was natural that he'd arrange an audition for another of the former American Blues players, Dusty Hill.

Joe Michael Hill, "Dusty," "The Dust," "Groover McToober," "Duster"—if anyone fit more than one nickname, it was Dusty Hill. He was born on May 19, 1949, in Dallas, and early in his youth one could see he was a natural born entertainer and future man of many talents, some more mentionable than others. His stepfather worked at a Ford plant and his real father was a truck driver whom he never knew too well. His mother, Myrl, worked as a waitress. He and his older brother Rocky were raised in modest surroundings in east Dallas in a neighborhood that was a cross between Dogpatch, Watts, and Spanish Harlem. To give you a clearer idea of what it was like, Dusty and his brother had the select pleasure of going to school with Richard Speck, later better known as the infamous Chicago mass murderer. Theirs was a tough neighborhood.

Dusty and Rocky were musically inclined from an early age. They grew up playing guitars and singing, and started playing beer joints before their teens. Their show-business instincts probably came from their mother, who brought home and enjoyed all types of music and was once a Bessie Smith–type blues singer. Being exposed to so much music, and constantly being around crowded beer joints, the Hill boys were raised playing music, entertaining, and often literally singing for their suppers.

Dusty's main musical influence and idol was always Elvis Presley. He even carried pictures of "The King" in his wardrobe case later on in his career. Years ago, during a moment of alcoholically induced candor, Dusty told me that he would be satisfied if he could sing and play bass like Paul McCartney. Hey, go for it, Dust! By now he ought to be satisfied with just being himself. He was able to use his voice and bass playing to go from the outhouse to the penthouse just like McCartney. The only difference today is the size of their penthouses.

When Dusty and Rocky got older they formed the Starliners and then the Deadbeats. At one time or another they sat in with different blues greats like Freddie King and Lightnin' Hopkins, and this is how they learned their blues chops. Eventually they met Frank, who was hanging out and jamming at the same clubs. As I said before, the three of them eventually formed the Warlocks, reincarnated into the American Blues, around 1967.

When Rocky, Dusty, and Frank played together, no matter what the name of the band, Dusty was the lead singer. Since they had to play clubs, they wound up doing a lot of "cover" songs which involved trying to sound *exactly* like the record. The American Blues had to be able to play all hits past and present, which meant that Dusty singing lead vocals had to emulate a remarkable range of different vocal styles. His high-pitched Little Anthony vocal for "Tears on My Pillow" (complete with vibrato) was so close to the real thing it was hysterical. He also did a great Johnny Cash, and of course, Elvis.

Playing in joints like the Cellars strengthened Dusty's skills, and I mean more than the musical. He regularly had to be prepared to deal with drunk hecklers in the crowd. Dusty became a pro at using humorous one-liners to calm down the rowdies, and this developed into an important ingredient of his eventual stage presence. The Cellar bistros were open until six in the morning. This meant that after musicians elsewhere finished their regular gigs they would head to the Cellar and jam until closing time. One of the main reasons Dusty is so versatile on bass and vocals is because he accompanied musicians with levels of skill that ranged from *great* to *oh, my god*. He also had to be able to play a wide assortment of material from reggae to rock and country to classical. Playing under these conditions—it may not have seemed like it at the time—offered excellent training.

After the American Blues broke up, Dusty and Frank (thankfully, I'd bet) dyed their hair back to normal colors. They played whatever gigs could be picked up. In one case Dusty and Frank did a tour with some other Dallas musicians as a bogus version of the Zombies. They toured the northern part of America and southern Canada booked into clubs as "the *real* Zombies from England." This meant that these teenaged Texans had to adopt fake British accents to keep from blowing their covers. If you've ever heard someone from Dallas try to imitate an Englishman, you can imagine how well they pulled that one off.

Bass-playing gigs were scarce after the Zombies tour. Dusty eventually found himself in Houston working for some friends of his who owned a small club called the Old Quarter. There was a room upstairs they let him use in exchange for services rendered, which were mainly tending bar and sweeping up the place. His bass playing talents were called on only if he went and jammed with somebody.

It was to this upstairs room that drumster Frank Beard took Billy Gibbons to meet Dusty for the first time in the latter part of 1969. Frank had finally set up the ZZ Top audition but without any warning to Dusty. Dusty struggled awake with a crashing hangover, and from the vantage point of a mattress dumped on the floor, learned that he was meeting the guy he needed to impress a few hours later with his bass playing and musicianship. The encounter was understandably brief. Billy had no reason to think that this bleary drunk was anything more than another would-be musician.

Dusty told me that he arrived some hours afterward at the club designated for the audition via some car he had managed to hitch a ride in. He was carrying nothing but a well-used bass that I think he may have borrowed. Ham and Gibbons had also asked another bass player to audition at the same time; this guy drove up in a fancy sports car, stepped out in designer fashions, and removed a gleaming, brand-new bass from his trunk. This guy projected an image like he was "Mr. Cooltone" in the flesh, and Dusty later admitted to being a tad intimidated.

But Dusty had one thing going for him that Cooltone was missing: Frank. While the ultra-cool bass player was doing his audition, Frank used the old Ethridge technique of playing sloppy to make Cooltone sound bad. Dusty also tried to help out his own situation by sitting at a table near Ham and doing magic tricks with a cigarette to divert his attention. Dusty won the job, but I suspect it may have been a split decision.

It was at this point that ZZ Top suddenly began to be a band that reached out and really grabbed your attention. Once Dusty was plugged in as the permanent bass player, a style and sound had been created that was unique and all its own. The blues-rooted musicianship each of the members had acquired during their individual musical experiences jelled to form a remarkable combination.

Billy, Frank, and Dusty had to constantly write and rehearse; inspiration always has its companion, perspiration. At this time all of their equipment was stored in the garage at Billy's parents' house, where Billy lived, so this became the convenient place to practice. Convenient for the band members, that is! Billy's parents and everyone in the vicinity had to develop a tolerance for it all. However, Billy's dad was very understanding, since he played music for a living, too, and the neighbors eventually gave up complaining to the police. Everybody resigned themselves to listening to a future international rock and roll attraction get itself in gear—ZZ Top had finally found that magic chemistry, and hopefully it would explode "Texas Boogie" onto the music scene with the intensity of one of Dan Mitchell's old flashpot charges.

3

"SHOW BIDNESS"

About the same time ZZ Top was beginning to *find* itself in late 1969, I was beginning to *lose* myself.

I had cruised into an important crossroad—starting college—but I had also encountered a "Road Closed Due To Major Repairs" sign. That's the price you pay when you spend more time surfing Gulf of Mexico waves than thinking about making class. I had this funny, empty feeling inside me. For want of a better analogy, I felt like I had awakened at midnight with a terrible hunger but wasn't sure what I wanted to eat. I found myself staring into what you might call the refrigerator of life, trying to decide on a tasty snack and at the same time hoping like hell that the snack wouldn't turn out to be mold-covered Spam laced with E-coli bacteria.

About the only thing I had going for me was the fact that I owned a van. Actually the *bank* owned it; I was merely making

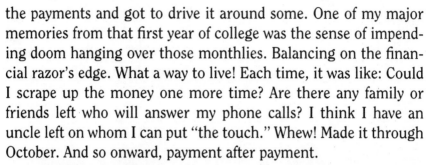

the payments and got to drive it around some. One of my major memories from that first year of college was the sense of impending doom hanging over those monthlies. Balancing on the financial razor's edge. What a way to live! Each time, it was like: Could I scrape up the money one more time? Are there any family or friends left who will answer my phone calls? I think I have an uncle left on whom I can put "the touch." Whew! Made it through October. And so onward, payment after payment.

In 1969, aiming to redirect myself, I decided to sit out a semester of college. Well, actually, I was on academic suspension from Del Mar University, if you want to get technical about it all. Now, I know it sounds stupid for me to have been on the verge of throwing away a perfectly good sheepskin in trade for a slice of West Coast Cosmic Consciousness, but surf fever was new to Texas and I had gotten totally caught up in it. Hell, the only reason I owned the van was to haul surfboards around in and on. But that surf van would turn out to be the most important thing I ever owned. It wound up changing my life.

Around the latter part of 1969, I was sitting at a friend's house helping him nurse some wounds via Acapulco Gold vapor therapy. This friend needed massive doses of such a universal cure-all, having done a Cuisinart number on his right leg recently: In an elevated mood, he unwisely decided to kick a parked car while exiting a freeway ramp on his chopper at high speed. The leg wound up on the back bumper, and I was now at his house amiably helping him inhale exotic fumes while we discussed our respective predicaments.

After an hour or so of diligent, therapeutic application of the vapors, we were joined by a couple of guys who immediately struck me as being "different." From their English-style T-shirts, bell-bottom pants, and pasty white complexions that rivaled that of a night-shift mortician, I could tell that they were most definitely *not* of the surfing persuasion. The guys' names were Pete Tickle and Ricky Staffacher. It turned out that they were something called roadies and worked for a band called ZZ Top. I wasn't quite sure what a roadie was (did they pick up road kill for the highway department?), but like everybody in Houston, I knew of ZZ Top. They were some new local band whose name sounded like it had been lifted from the brand of rolling papers that I had just finished using. I had even heard them play a couple of gigs, stories that I now related to Pete and Ricky.

The first time I saw ZZ Top was in Houston at the Coliseum; they were opening for Janis Joplin. She was the one I had gone to see, naturally, but ZZ Top definitely caught my attention. ZZ's bass player was still Billy Ethridge, but Frank Beard was the drummer by then. I knew him from his days with the American Blues, and I had gone to the beach with him that memorable morning when he still had blue hair. The thing I remembered most about ZZ Top was the intensity of the music and the advanced ability of ZZ's lead guitar player, my old schoolmate, Billy Gibbons. Billy was playing with a style that was unique and fascinating. His appearance was also an eye-catcher; with his long mane of reddish hair and red chinstrap beard sans moustache, Billy looked like a cross between the Cowardly Lion and a freaked-out Amish preacher. It was apparent at first sight that Billy Gibbons was going to make a mark in the music industry, if only for his over-the-edge looks.

However, this time it was Janis Joplin's show and she definitely upstaged ZZ. Janis and her band, Big Brother and the Holding Company, were not only great from an entertainment standpoint, but Janis also took time out to terrorize a fire marshall in the middle of her show. At the time there was a Sunday curfew of 11:00 P.M. at the Coliseum, and some cretinous bureaucrat made the mistake of walking out on stage during her rendition of "Ball and Chain." He had the audacity to tap Janis on her shoulder while she was singing and tell her that her time was up. *Janis Joplin's time was up?* No way; if anybody's, it was this moron's! Janis ripped her microphone from its stand, wound up, and let it fly like a major league pitcher. She nailed the fire marshal dead center in his chest and screamed at him to "GET OFF MY

29

FUCKIN' STAGE!" As the audience hooted, he promptly did just that, making the wise decision to let her finish her entire show rather than face another fireball. It was obvious that Janis would personally *kick* his ass if he did anything else but *haul* ass.

The other story I told these roadies was about the time I went to a club in Groves, Texas, over near Beaumont. Groves was a typical small east Texas community, and the club occupied what used to be a grocery store. An older gentleman by the name of Bob Westbury had converted it into a rock music haven called the Town House(!), and the crowd that frequented it was comprised of small-town country teenagers with big-town rock and roll tastes. They were very enthusiastic about their music, and the packed room was charged with raging hormones and youthful energy and excitement.

The most notable thing about this show, aside from the fact that the dressing room was appropriately located in what used to be the meat locker, was that this would be the last ZZ Top show before Dusty Hill was brought on to play bass. The bass player for this show was Mike Johnson, who frequently sat in during the transition period after Billy Ethridge, but Dusty was on the horizon. At this show I registered on the fact that there was no keyboard player around. "Salt Lick," the tune that first got me interested in ZZ Top, definitely had organ parts. I had noticed the missing instrument the other time I saw ZZ, but didn't give it as much thought then. I would find out later that Lanier Greig played keys for the record. After Lanier's time, Billy had to learn to play a guitar part for live shows that sounded close to the keyboard part on the record.

After I told these two roadies about my peripheral experiences with ZZ Top, they talked about their much more direct involvement. They were getting ready for an upcoming show in Fort Worth and were bitching about the high cost of renting a van in which to haul the band's equipment. Not only that, ZZ's manager, Bill Ham, insisted that they get the van back immediately after the concert, so as to save paying for a second rental day.

A dim light flickered on in the back of my brain. *I* had a maxivan for surfing purposes, and it was too cold to surf. . . . Right then and there I offered the use of my van and my personal services as a stevedore at a cost equal to only one-half of what a rental company would charge. Why not check out this rock and roll "roadie" business, have a few laughs, and *get paid* for doing it? I'd love it, the bank would love it, the relatives I was bleeding for cash would be ecstatic and might put me back on their Christmas card list. Here was a no-lose scenario.

Pete and Ricky took me up on the deal right there, knowing that Bill Ham would go for it. By the next morning, I was scheduled to pick up my new acquaintances and all the ZZ Top equipment on the morning of the concert. We would drive to Fort Worth, do the show, then take turns driving back down to Houston afterwards. No problem.

I had no idea that my wheels, and that deal, were starting me off down the pothole-filled road towards fifteen years of rock and roll. Historians have a word for it: *contingency*. All actions are led up to by unplanned accidents. It was the unique combination of owning a surf van, knowing the friend who knew the roadies, my assistance with the friend's vapor therapy, and being there at the right time that put me on the road with ZZ Top.

Who knows? If I'd gone someplace else that night, I might be writing about Jimmy Swaggert today.

The next weekend, after I cut the van deal with ZZ Top's two roadies, I more or less became one myself. My first gig was in Fort Worth at a redneck watering hole called Panther Hall. On this auspicious occasion it was the hippies who were out in full force. The rednecks were out of sight, probably hiding in the shadows waiting to ambush an unsuspecting flower child and sheep-shear his locks off. The talent lineup for the show, dropping back from the closing act (better known as the headliner) to the opening act (better known as the opener), was:

FEVER TREE
with special guest
SAVOY BROWN
featuring
APHRODITE
and also
ZZ TOP

A person who is unfamiliar with "show bidness," as I would later hear Bill Ham pronounce it, might not be aware of the critical importance of positioning an act on the talent lineup, or marquee. Consider it safe to say that some performers would mull over giving away their first-born child just to move up a notch on the bill. Imagine what would be sacrificed for the *top* spot.

As far as rock and roll concert billing is concerned, here's the pecking order. You have the "headliner," the "co-headliner," the "special guest," the "special appearance by," the "appearance by special arrangement," the "featured guest attraction," the plain old "featuring," and . . . your "also's." The absolute pits in the entertainment industry is finding yourself grouped in with the "also's." A band manager will do anything to avoid this curse and the stigma that goes with it.

In the music industry the positioning of talent in the lineup is usually worked out weeks in advance. It is based on various guidelines, such as an act's current album sales, its status in certain regions of the country, its drawing power in certain cities, how much an act can bleed off a once popular name, what favors are owed to an act, what favors an act owes, how much money under the table has been generated, what future kickbacks are being promised, the quantity of drugs an act has given away, and/or how many blowjobs have been handed out. For this Fort Worth show, Bill Ham was obviously running a little lean in all these caregories. ZZ Top was a dead last "also."

But it didn't matter. As was soon to become his pattern, Ham used "show bidness" savvy and Texas street smarts to make up for whatever weaknesses he might have had in tangible trade-offs. In other words, he lied his ass off.

It happened to be snowing that night, not a common occurrence in central Texas, and Ham and the band showed up late for the show. Ham's excuses to the promoter pointed out the dangerous driving conditions through which the band had struggled, also that it had been necessary to stop and get a hand warmer for his lead guitar player so that he could unfreeze his fingers and be able to play. You could almost hear the violin music playing in the background as Ham spun his woeful tale. He gave his assurance that if Aphrodite opened the show instead of ZZ, Billy's fingers would have time to thaw and ZZ could be ready to play by the time the other band left the stage. Right! That night I was privileged to witness twin miracles: the miraculous flash-thawing of Billy's fingers, and Bill Ham's miraculous jump-shifting of ZZ in the talent lineup without pissing off the promoter enough to throw them off the show entirely.

As I watched ZZ Top for the first time as a backstage participant, I noticed something about the three band members. They had a rare combination of talent and spontaneous musical improvisation, and it was obvious that each of them enjoyed the hell out of the unique sound they were creating. With the arrival of Dusty Hill the missing piece of the puzzle had been inserted. This wasn't just my opinion; everybody else in the hall felt the same way. The volatile mixture of talents in ZZ Top lit up the audience and it responded with tremendous approval. ZZ Top completely stole the show. The kids knew they were in the presence of a new and unique sound combining blues and rock with a certain Texas flamboyance. What was it? Their new style of music, their stage presence, their sincerity, or just plain magic? That night it drove the people who had come to see them wild. Out of all the lineup of talent, ZZ Top was the band that was remembered.

After Panther Hall, without any formal agreement, it was just assumed that I would continue as Bill Ham's trucking company of choice for the band. I was, clearly, the cheapest transportation available in Houston. I started riding from show to show on weekends or more often as needed, taking the two permanent ZZ crew members, Ricky and Pete, wherever ZZ was to next appear. I was fascinated with the workings of the entertainment industry, Ham's "show bidness." Plans for returning to college after the period of absence insisted upon by Del Mar's administration began to seem less pressing. After all, I didn't really know why I had been in school anyway. By hauling ZZ Top's equipment around, I was earning enough money to handle the van payments and still have a fair amount left over. Gradually I realized that at least for the moment, this was what I wanted to do full-time. Hell, I was practically an entrepreneur.

Rock and roll is the contemporary version of the circus. Certain little boys, with wanderlust in their blood and curiosity in their hearts, can still run away to it. With no questions and no doubts, I joined ZZ Top's rock and roll caravan and was on my way. The direction in which I was moving was unimportant.

Just one thing, however. I didn't appreciate it at the time, but the Panther Hall gig with a crowd of two or three thousand was really bigtime compared to some of the ZZ Top appearances the future held in store. Standard fare was every dump where a few bucks could be earned. I soon would realize that "show bidness" can be a pretty fickle mistress.

PART II

RUNNIN'
SMOOTH

4

FROM LOW-BUDGET
TO LEGENDARY

A couple of months after that first big night at Panther Hall, Ham got the band into a memorably forgettable gig. "Win ZZ Top for a Day" was a promotion that some Houston radio station thought was a good idea. That fact alone should have sent up the red flags. The contest prize was a party, featuring live music by ZZ, to which the winner could invite fifty of his or her closest friends. Ham was taking whatever jobs for the band he could get in order to give them exposure to the masses, no matter how infinitesimal the mass of masses might be, as well as to generate a little cash flow. Consequently when he booked the Boys a gig you never knew what to expect.

It's not so bad nowadays, but back in the early seventies one of the first things you could count on was this: If a radio station tried to do the production for a show all by itself, without the help of the band or a promoter, you could rest assured that something (or everything) was going to be totally fucked up. The case of "Win ZZ Top for a Day" was proof positive of this.

The "happening spot" was a small meeting room off the main concourse of a big shopping mall in Houston. Sounds good? No way. This party room closely resembled a concrete blockhouse. The walls were made of cinder blocks and the floor was polished cement. If you'd put a drain in the middle, hung a tire from a rope, and put bars on one side it would have made a dandy primate cage. Such ingredients are not exactly conducive to perfecto acoustic quality. The place echoed like an oversized shower stall.

To top things off, the poor schmuck who won the band was only fourteen years old, and either the kid didn't have any friends to invite or he was too shy to invite the few he had. Moreover, the kid's parents dropped him off and then headed into the mall to do a little bargain-hunting. Not a single soul besides the kid had showed up by "party time."

Under the circumstances most bands would have packed up and left, but not ZZ. The band felt sorry for the little guy and played anyway. This streak of humanity was a trait Billy, Frank, and Dusty would retain throughout their careers. They had compassion for their fans and felt duty-bound to deliver their music to the best of their ability, no matter what size the crowd. This time they even asked the crew to go on a search-and-seizure mission throughout the mall to try and find some likely candidates to come to the party. A few kids were finally recruited, Cokes were sent for because the radio station hadn't thought (or were too cheap) to provide any, and in general the band tried to make the best of a situation that seemed doomed from the start.

At a "show" like this ZZ tended more to rehearse than to perform, but this wasn't bad. The Boys' rehearsals were often more entertaining than a regular show. This was because they would play material they couldn't do at regular appearances, when they needed to play their own original music. For rehearsals they could dust off all the oldies but goodies they had cut their musical teeth on. In a casual situation like "Win ZZ Top for a

Day," the crew would sometimes join in on percussion instruments. It was not unusual for Pete or Ricky to sneak behind the speaker stacks and do their "dance of the nekkid maracas" for the band's amusement.

I didn't want to do a strip behind the speakers for this particular party, but I did get into the act once at a club in Fort Worth called the Circus. Overly influenced by an adrenaline rush produced by rock and roll fever, I intentionally set my blue jeans on fire with lighter fluid and then boogied out from behind Billy's speaker stacks to hand him a towel during a break between songs. I damn near burned my leg off for the sake of rock and roll. Since it blew the minds of some people in the front row who were tripping on LSD, I was satisfied.

The whole "Win ZZ Top for a Day" farce turned out to be an unexpected success due to the band's sheer determination to give that kid a party. Everybody's opinion was that it might be his last, but by the end of the day the kid at least looked happier than he had when he arrived. Who knows; it might well have marked the start of a nerd recovery.

Things came to an end, however, when the kid's parents finished their shopping spree. They picked him up without even coming inside to see what their son had won, and left.

I hope that out there somewhere there is a *former* nerd with a fond memory of owning ZZ Top for a day. As for those radio station promoters who never even checked on how things were going, I hope they wound up hustling the ratings on Alaska's north slope.

So you can see that rock and roll is not all glamour and glitz. Rest assured that for every star-studded L.A. Forum gig a band might get to play there are fifty like the one ZZ did for the nerd. In the early days before MTV was around, it usually took several years of heavy touring before an act could become an "overnight sensation." During that time it was inevitable that you would be sub-jected to some nightmare venues.

Pancho's was an almost-nightmare.

This particular show was a 1971 New Year's Eve bash held at the world-famous rock and roll emporium and ptomaine palace in Tyler, Texas, known as Pancho's Mexican Cafeteria. Some frat rats had rented the restaurant and the band for the night and they intended to ring in the New Year in style. For those of you who may not know much about Texas geography and lore, Tyler is located in a "dry" county and Pancho's was a cheap Mexican food cafeteria—not your basic main ingredients for a kickass New Year's Eve.

Our gear had to be moved into Pancho's through a maze of chairs and tables, and then wedged into a small corner that the frat rats had designated as the bandstand. It was more suited for a one-man band than a power trio, and even he would have been cramped. It's a good thing that we were flexible and had brought only a small part of the usual equipment, because there was barely enough juice in the place to run what gear we had along. If the normal array of amplifiers had been plugged in and switched on there would have been an instant brownout all across that part of Tyler. To make matters worse, we were right next to the food line and had to look at greasy-brown guacamole and smell cardboard enchiladas all night, which was topped off with the blow of being in part of the bone dry, Bible-thumping South. Pros such as us could deal with sharing the spotlight with guacamole and enchi-ladas, but it was downright unbearable to think of not hoisting a few cold ones (or even hot ones) to celebrate the arrival of the New Year.

Thankfully, the frat rats did what they do best and smuggled in some booze. By the second set a party atmosphere kicked in despite the ambience of the *nachtlokal*. The band played a com-bination of original material along with other hits, and the crowd loved the mixture. As always, everybody had a great time because ZZ made it that way. After a few shots 'n' beers, I even got to like the handy placement of the guac' and enchiladas. If you overlooked the way they looked, smelled, and tasted, they weren't all that bad.

The reputation of ZZ Top at this point was spreading by word of mouth, largely due to successful gigs like Pancho's. But even though they made the best of it, I don't think the Boys in the band were too thrilled about playing New Year's Eve spots in a dry county or sharing the limelight with rapidly aging Mexican food. ZZ never played another cafeteria, and it damned sure didn't play another local-option county where the option had gone the wrong way.

In the early days of ZZ Top's career—'70, '71, and '72—the band was part of many unusual marquee matchups. This was so the almighty dollar return would be maximized. Now, I don't begrudge promoters for trying to make a buck, and I can't blame Bill Ham for trying to put ZZ in front of as many people as possible, but from time to time the combinations got a little ridiculous. Sometimes they weren't even close. ZZ once played a show with Osibisa, a black African drum group, plus the stand-up comedians Cheech and Chong. That's stretching market demographics to the limit.

In 1971 ZZ did a tour in the Northeast as the opening act for the English psychedelic rock band Uriah Heep and the American rhythm and soul band Earth, Wind, and Fire. Ponder that mix for a minute! The crowds in these instances were a mixture of acid heads, soul brothers, and cratered-out biker fans of ZZ Top. There were fights before, during, or after every show. Observing the audience follies from the relative safety of the stage provided nightly sport for all of us. ZZ's music was starting to become popular with what appeared to be a rough and unsavory element of society. In fact, the crowds attracted were so consistently rowdy that at one point several colleges considered blackballing ZZ from performing in certain arenas. Fortunately, it never happened.

A favorite matchup of mine about this time was in San Antonio at a club called the Jam Factory. ZZ was opening for The One and Only Fats Domino. Ham had arranged it so that the band could also play a set *after* Fats did his One and Only Show. Being the wily manager that he is, always hoping to move the Boys up a notch or two on the talent lineup, Ham hoped that it would appear to the people who came in late that Fats Domino was the opening act for ZZ Top! Ham was always scheming, trying to gain ZZ an edge.

Billy, Dusty, and Frank were pumped up, nervous, and proud all at once to be appearing on the same stage with a legend like Fats, but the show turned out to be nothing but trouble. For starters, it being San Antonio, the crowd was primarily made up of Hispanic gents and ladies who had come only to see Fats. They did *not* want to sit through some relatively unknown act, which of course is exactly what ZZ was at the time. The minute ZZ Top walked on stage the crowd began to hoot and holler for Fats; Billy and Dusty hadn't even plugged in their guitars yet, a bad sign.

When Billy Gibbons *did* plug in his guitar . . . nothing happened. His amplifiers were deader than a truck-struck weasel.

Billy had been more nervous than a white-collar criminal in a cell full of bikers to start with, but when he found out his amps didn't work, he lost it. He fumbled around with the knobs on his equipment, tried to look "musician cool," mumbled something into his mike about technical problems, then led Frank and Dusty off the stage and back to the sanctuary of the dressing room. I need hardly say that the brief public service announcement did not go down well with the hot-blooded San Antonians. They didn't want to hear anything ZZ Top had to offer in the first place, and they sure as shit didn't want to wait around for the band to get its electrical act together. Shouts, catcalls, and an occasional whistle rang out across the auditorium, and the ugliness threshold was low.

Since Ricky Staffacher had left the roadie business, Pete Tickle and I were the "technicians" responsible for making the jumble of equipment work. We frantically ran around the stage checking plugs, cables, patchcords, junction boxes, and—Oh, yeah—the amps, dude!

The Boys were watching all this from the dressing room. It looked like genuine bad news. Billy had taken the lead in yanking off his usual footwear and lacing on tennis shoes, Frank and Dusty hastily following suit. They had all been in nasty crowd situations before, and if it came down to showing assholes and elbows, they knew from bitter experience that your effectiveness in hauling ass in a pair of Tony Lamas is close to zip. By changing their footwear they at least were giving themselves a fighting chance at survival.

I don't remember how or why—wise technicians never ask too many questions—but suddenly under our hands the amps miraculously came back on. Now what in the . . . ? Well, on with the show. We called the band back to the stage, and the boys came on glancing warily around. The audience response on their second appearance was reminiscent of a Saturday afternoon in ancient Rome at the old Coliseum. It was Lions 2, Christians 0, and the masses were howling for the Lions to kick some more Christian butt. Shakey, but nonetheless undaunted, ZZ Top took the stage ready to do its best to boogie down at full tilt.

One small problem, however: Billy plugged in again, switched on again . . . and again, nothing happened. Have mercy!

This time, instead of immediately leaving the stage, Billy tried to make light of the situation. He cracked a few nervous jokes about the unpredictable nature of electricity, attempting to persuade the crowd that the problem with his amp would soon be fixed. The bullets of sweat beading on his forehead betrayed his weak attempt at sincerity, but it didn't matter, anyway. The impatient audience couldn't have cared less.

Loud voices with thick Mexican accents started yelling from various places in the crowd, which now looked and acted more like a mob than anything else. "Geet a badder waan, maan! Joo chood geet a *new* waan!" Peering out at them twisting and simmering in the dimness beyond the footlights, I appreciated what Travis and Bowie and Crockett must have felt like at sunrise on the Alamo's final day.

Billy just couldn't win. He was Baron Frankenstein trying to convince the torch-bearing citizens not to burn down his castle, and got about the same degree of favorable reaction. All Billy could do was lead the band back to the dressing room looking like a starting pitcher headed for the showers at the top of the first inning.

What a night. The *best* crowd response came later when Fats Domino stood up and bumped his grand piano all the way across the stage during "When the Saints Come Marching In." The *next best* crowd response went to Pete and me when we started taking ZZ's equipment down after the band's second disorderly retreat. The cheers and hollering weren't much of a consolation prize. At least no organic matter came whistling down on us as we worked.

ZZ did manage to pull off playing the second set, but only after Pete and I drove clear across San Antonio at a hundred miles an hour to borrow an amp for Billy to use. The show the Boys wound up doing after Fats left the stage lacked the usual ZZ punch, and Ham's candle of one-upsmanship had burned to a sorry stub. The evening had been rear-ended by the gremlins of electricity.

There was another marvelous matchup near Atlanta at a place called Lake Spivey. We were booked on a two-act outdoor show and the act ZZ was opening for was Ike and Tina Turner. Needless to say, the crowd was predominantly black. ZZ had better luck at this show, however. Gibbons by now had gotten a *"new* waan" and the amps worked perfectly. The Ike and Tina audience accepted and enjoyed ZZ's blues-rooted rock music. Even though ZZ was obviously some white boys trying to play the blues, the crowd of ten thousand appreciated the sincerity with which the music was delivered. This time ZZ didn't need to lace up their running shoes, and even got to do an encore. Some more fans were signed up, and overall the outcome was good.

After ZZ was finished, Pete and I packed the gear in record time so that we could catch most of Ike and Tina's show. Since we worked for the opening act, we naturally had total stage area access, and I took full advantage of it. I sat on the ground at dead stage center, directly under Tina's microphone location, and (by accident) had the pleasure of looking straight up her dress for the entire show. Hot damn, Tina!

While I was checking out Tina's costume, *Billy* was checking out what Ike and his band members were wearing. He continually studied black entertainers and their style nuances, and always tried to stay on top of any new musical or fashion statements, "dat might be hap'-NIN'," with the brothers. "He be tryin' to stay hip, you dig?" It was an important influence on Billy's tunes and lyrics, and a major influence on his stage "look."

Billy flipped out when he saw what Ike and his band wore onto that stage. The brothers were sporting skin-tight shorts called hot pants, mid-calf lace-up boots, panty hose, and turtle-neck sweaters. On the black guys it looked superhip. Gibbons *had* to have an outfit just like it. He forgot to consider the fact that he was a honky, and a red-headed one at that.

When he got back to Houston, Billy went on an all-day shopping spree trying to find a pair of hot pants that would fit him. I'd have given a lot to see the faces of the women's apparel salesladies when he asked them where he could go to try on his selections. After he finally got the entire ensemble together it had taken so much effort that he was bound and determined to wear it all for the next show regardless of how it looked.

The next show, where the new "Billy the brother" look was to be revealed to an astonished world, was in Memphis, Tennessee. Ham had lined up an opener for the Allman Brothers Band. ZZ had done shows with the Allmans prior to this one, and there was

45

a great mutual respect between the two bands and crews. We were always up for a show with them.

The very first time ZZ Top played with the Allmans had come about through Ham's contacts with a West Coast promoter named Irving Granz. ZZ was booked on a four-city Southern tour. The first show had ZZ opening for the psychedelic San Francisco group Quicksilver Messenger Service and a jazz-pop horn band from the Chicago area calling itself Chase. Once again a promoter had organized a show across a ridiculously broad musical spectrum, but we were used to it by now. We'd better have been, since the three shows afterward included the Allman Brothers Band as well.

This was a meeting that the Boys had been looking forward to ever since the Allmans' first album came out. Billy had heard Duane Allman play and wanted to meet him. There was strong competition between most bands at that time, and everybody always wondered whether one band could blow away another. ZZ Top blew most bands away, but the Allmans were powerful and a real challenge. The first show with the Allmans was to be in New Orleans, one of ZZ's favorite places to play; the next was going to be in Houston, ZZ's hometown.

In New Orleans the show was at the infamous Warehouse, a 3,000-seat club in an old nineteenth-century cotton warehouse. It always had a steamy, funky, GET DOWN atmosphere with a crowd of hot-blooded coon-ass guys and sultry Cajun queens generally at redline intensity. ZZ got the crowd all lathered up with just their opening set, and there were still three acts to go. Chase was up next, using ZZ's equipment for the gig since after their previous night's show a wiseguy had pissed in the gas tank of Chase's equipment bus, which consequently never made it to New Orleans. Then came the Allmans. Hearing them crank into their opening song, "Statesboro Blues," was an unforgetable moment for all of us. They were musically tight and magically powerful. Billy, Dusty, and Frank left before Quicksilver played. Nothing could have topped the Allmans for them.

I mention all this because Duane Allman's guitar technique seriously influenced Billy Gibbons. The next night, when ZZ played Houston, I remember noticing subtle changes in Billy's playing style. He slowed down a touch, became more precise in his fretting, played fewer but tastier notes, and delivered one of the best sets he ever played.

As it turned out, ZZ was lucky to be on the Houston show at all. Irving Granz had been considering scratching us from the bill because he felt that four bands were one too many. Ham was popping arteries at the possibility of ZZ not getting to play Houston, the Boys' hometown. But after the *piss*adventure with Chase's bus, they got scratched instead. There you have the element of luck in the music business again. If somebody's bladder had been sending less urgent messages, and that somebody's sense of humor had been such that unloading on the side of the bus would have been enough, there would have been a different photo on the back cover of ZZ's *Rio Grande Mud* album, because that picture was taken at the Houston show.

So now, roughly six months after Houston, ZZ was in Memphis, about to musically duel the Allmans once more. It was the first time ZZ had played with the Allmans since that minitour, and the bandsmen wanted to be in top form. To this end, Billy insisted on wearing his brand-new Ike and Tina soul brother hot pants outfit. Frank and Dusty were none too thrilled about his decision, since they had to share the stage with a guy who looked like he had made a weak attempt at cross-dressing, but they had to go along with it. When Billy got it into his mind to do something, he was going to do it no matter what.

When ZZ took the stage, and those ol' Memphis boys in the audience got a good look at Billy in his hot pants and pantyhose, well, it was like Saturday night in a border town topless bar. We're talking wolf whistle and catcall city. Billy was also going through a short hair, de-bearded, de-moustached, bespectacled phase at the time. Envision a pale white honky with short reddish hair, totally clean-shaven, wearing black horn-rimmed glasses and

47

stuffed into his new raiment. He was trying to pull off playing boogie and blues while looking like Woody Allen in drag. The audience was roaring with hilarity at the sight, but it was the sort of wild cheerfulness that is occasionally associated with a thrown long-neck beer bottle or two whistling through the air toward the stage.

Undaunted, Billy broke into ZZ's opener, an instrumental that was simply called "C-shuffle" but would later be reworked, given words, and renamed "Thunderbird." Later on in the 90s a group from Austin called the Nighthawks attempted to sue ZZ over the rights to "Thunderbird," claiming they wrote it first. As far as I know the results are still pending. But in the early years this powerhouse shuffle would be one of ZZ's best known live tunes, until "La Grange" came along. It was a serious attention-getter, and that night in Memphis was no different than anywhere else it has been played. The catcalls and wolf whistles evaporated instantly and the audience went totally berserk. I guess you can't hide good music, no matter how ridiculous the musician's costume. Billy played his ass off that night, driving straight on from "C-shuffle" into the rest of the act. Wearing a getup like the one he was modeling, I guess he figured he'd better not let up the pace for a second for fear that one of the audience might rush the stage and try to stick a dollar bill in his hot pants.

During the set, three of the Allman Brothers Band—Duane Allman, Barry Oakley, and Dickie Betts—came over to the side of the stage to follow what was happening. I had met Duane before, and during a break in the lighting cues I went over to talk with him. I felt that I had to apologize for Gibbons' attire. I told Duane about the gig with Ike and Tina, and that after Billy saw Ike's band he went temporarily insane. Duane had a great appreciation for Billy and had even told me on a prior occasion that Gibbons was one of the best guitar players he had ever heard.

Duane was a class act and just laughed at my apology.

"That's okay, baby," he said. "All of us git-tar players are a little crazy."

I turned to look out at Billy raging and howling in his hot pants, the crowd of Memphians roaring their approval of him, and thought about how close genius is to madness. With Billy, you always had to wonder which side of the line he was on, or if a line even existed in his case. And if it did, could he really *choose* where he stood?

Let me finish off this chapter with a final example of low-budget giggin' days.

It hadn't taken me long to learn that to survive as a rock and roll roadie you had to be able to adapt to all kinds of unexpected (and sometimes expected) problems. No matter how well you *thought* you'd planned things in advance, more times than not something was going to come up that you just plain forgot to consider. Since there wasn't a great deal of advanced technical planning in the ZZ organization in these early days, the road crew had to become adapting sumbitches.

Not only did we have to come up with solutions for the unsolvable, most of the time this was accomplished while performing deeds way up and beyond the call of duty. There could be electrical problems, stage space problems, problems with other bands and crews, access problems, stagehand problems (if we had any helpers, which was rare), crowd problems—the list goes on. It's hard to imagine a single show presenting *every* possible problem all at once, but I had the rare privilege of living through one. This happened near Santa Fe, New Mexico, in the winter of '71.

In these early touring days Ham was trying to do a juggling act between managing ZZ Top and fulfilling the demands of his promotions job at Daily's. He had no time to prepare an itinerary for us. This meant that there wasn't enough notice on some shows to even find out the name of the city we were going to before we left for it. It was just, "Head for Denver, boy, and keep on phonin'!"

49

The particular show I've been leading up to was, according to Bill Ham, in Santa Fe. This was not the case by any means. It was early afternoon when we found out from some locals there that the place we were supposed to be was in Española, a small town *near* Santa Fe. That's if you call thirty or forty miles "near."

We had been driving icy mountain roads all night and part of the day. This in itself would tend to generate a little anxiety. Driving a Ryder "yellow dog" truck in the mountains in winter ice and snow ain't no carnival pony ride. Being too tired to drive and too scared to sleep, Pete and I were in less than optimal condition. We both felt like we'd been swallered by a buzzard and puked onto a cactus plant, and we couldn't wait to get to the club ZZ was playing so we could warm our hands and feet, which were frozen due to the absence of an effective truck heater.

Finally we spotted the right street. So what if it had a few chuck holes in it? Our hearts raced like a two-stroke engine as we turned onto it and approached the block hosting Española's night-life district. Visions of hot coffee, or maybe even hot toddies by a blazing fire, raced through our brains. The gig was still ahead of us, but at least we would be off the road and warm.

But what was this? We wiped away moisture on the windshield to make certain our eyes weren't deceiving us. The houses and other buildings on either side of the street were changing from well-kept into hovels and rattraps. With each passing block we went further down the economic scale, until from middle class suburban U.S.A. we had warped into East Beirut in a drizzling rain. It was like going from color to black and white. I guess we were ready for it when we finally pulled up in front of the "club." There it was: a sheet metal quonset hut. An old and rusty one at that. I'm sure that in its heyday it made a dandy place to lube up a crop duster, but a rock and roll showcase club it wasn't. Ham had finally topped Pancho's for finding dives. This one didn't even come equipped with cardboard enchiladas.

After we regained our composure a little, we mustered up enough energy to walk inside and try to warm up. Unfortunately, inside was at least twenty degrees colder than outside. This phenomenon was made possible by the unique insulating qualities of bare, sheet metal walls and a concrete floor. The place was like a big meat locker, except for the fact that meat kept here would have been subjected to instant freezer burn.

The building seemed empty except for a piece of machinery that was sprawled in the middle of the floor with some legs sticking out of it. The machine turned out to be one of two building heaters, neither of which were working. The legs belonged to the owner of the place. He was trying to earnestly—and as it turned out, futilely—fix the heater before show time.

The owner was a middle-aged Hispanic-Native American whose face looked like it had been on the losing end of tribal tomahawk practice for many moons. We skeptically asked Plays-With-Machinery to explain exactly what the place was supposed to be. With pride he told us that it was to be a new night spot for the local kids to go instead of clubs in Santa Fe, which were prejudiced toward them.

Now here was a new one indeed! ZZ was going to be playing right in the middle of Injun Territory! Well, at least we'd made it to the right spot at last. We had a gig to do, it was getting late, we were professionals, by God, and now it was time to go to work. Cold or no cold, we were ready to rock. We asked where the stage was located.

Plays-With-Machinery pointed straight up.

We looked, and there, looming high above us, was a tiny loft that looked like it might be big enough to hold a traveling preacher who was passing through town lecturing on the demons of firewater. That was supposed to be the stage. It was connected to the ground floor by way of a narrow, crazy, twisting stairway from Hell. It looked like it was we who were going to be in need of a preacher.

There was no point in arguing. Pete and I somberly began to move the gear up those treacherous stairs. We didn't waste breath asking for help. It was obvious that there was only one chief, and no Indians were in sight.

An hour or so later, after we had bandaged up all the fingers smashed lugging speaker cabinets up, up, and up, and were taking a breather, one minor detail started to become apparent. ZZ's gear wouldn't fit the dimensions of the loft. Pete and I looked at each other with identical "Oh shit, I thought *you* measured it!" looks on our faces. At this juncture in time, exhausted and frozen, neither of us had been pegging the needle on Life's IQ meter.

By now it was getting late, so we had to make a snap decision as to the next best place to fit the gear. This was a foregone conclusion. Based on available electrical outlets and overall space needed, we had no choice but to set up right in the middle of the dance floor and directly in front of the only access to the lavatories. This meant that people would literally have to squeeze by the band and behind the speaker cabinets in order to answer nature's calls. Time was running out; we had to hope that Billy, Dusty, and Frank were prepared to have an "up-close and personal" relationship with the indigenous fans. It's not often that an entertainer has to step to one side in the middle of his act so that people can make it past him to the johns.

We tapped some reservoir of strength and wrestled the gear back down those stairs to ground level without opening too many of our previously acquired gashes. We also brought down some old wooden platforms from up there with which we improvised a stage. The end result was a miniature playing surface sixteen feet wide, eight feet deep, and *four inches* high.

Once the "stage" was completed, we powered together the sound system, amp-speaker stacks, and drums, all of which took some time. The band's gear had now become impressive by any standards, since Ham had arranged financing from the Daily's for brand-new equipment. ZZ was now backed by six Marshall amp-speaker stacks and one of the first sets of Fibes clear plastic drums. The lighting consisted of four garden-variety floodlights, two red and two blue, which were carefully trained on the setup.

When all was said and done, especially considering that the gear was in the middle of the dance floor instead of up in the loft, it looked very imposing.

The opening act for ZZ arrived. Yep, you guessed it: local talent every one. There was Plays-With-Drumsticks, Plays-With-Fender, Plays-With-Harmonica, and Plays-With-Himself, who I figured was their roadie. Most probably they all were related to Plays-With-Machinery.

As the band hauled its own modest assemblage of well-used gear up into the loft, eyeballing our stuff the whole way, the hostility and contempt felt for intruders was palpable. Prejudice runs both ways, you know. Battle lines were being drawn whether we liked it or not, and Pete and I were the only White Eyes in the vicinity. Pretending not to notice, we busied ourselves around the gear and stuck to ZZ turf.

The audience began to arrive. Yep, they were all tough-looking, and all ethnic.

These young people looked as if they remembered who it was that had broken every treaty since Columbus and were ready for a payback. Since the broken heaters had never been fixed, everybody in the crowd had on an overcoat or a blanket. All eyes darted back and forth between our equipment and Pete and me, including our luxurious shoulder-length hippie hairstyles. Where in the hell were Ham and the Boys? All kidding aside, these were poor people who resented what had been done to them by the Anglos over the years, and with reason. Being alone in the middle of them was not an uplifting experience.

Not waiting for the headliner, or for any introduction, the opening act began to play. They were awful. The people in the audience, a near-sellout crowd forty to fifty strong, stood around with their hands in their coat pockets or under their blankets. It was so cold inside the place that you could see your breath in the air, and all they were doing was trying to stay warm.

In the middle of their show the leader of the local band, who looked and talked like Cheech, started making sarcastic comments about ZZ. Speaking from the loft, he gazed down upon our gear from on high and addressed the fans. Forgive me if I try to present *exactly* what he said.

"The ZZ Tops are beeg, maan. Just loook at the chiney new geer. All *I* got ees thees leetle Fender amp, maan; but I can play the *chit* out of eet! Wee'll see how beeg the ZZ Tops are later, maan." Then he said something in their native tongue that caused the crowd to laugh hysterically and then look over at us with narrow-eyed smiles. Maybe he was imitating the way *we* talked! Who knows?

During the intermission, Plays-With-Machinery—who also talked like Cheech—went up to the loft and made a speech about the future of his little nightspot. He wanted all of his patrons to take an active part in the club, because it was going to be "their plaize" and not his. He told them that he was going to hang up a suggestion box, which he hoped they would fill with their ideas for the club and requests for future band appearances.

"Joo wan' the Rullin' Stuns, maan? I'll geet joo the Rullin' Stuns. Joo wan' the Moody Bloose, maan? I'll geet joo the Moody Bloose. Eet's joor plaize!"

He also exhorted them to suggest names for "their plaize." After a beat, a voice came forth from the frosty mist at the back and one of the tribe said, with total sincerety and chattering teeth, "How 'bout callin' eet the Refreegerator, maan?" Not one person laughed.

About this time ZZ Top arrived, much to Pete's and my relief. The last thing we needed was for them to be late. My relief was only temporary, though, because I had forgotten that ZZ's appearance tended to draw more than just casual notice. Billy walked in with his lion's mane and beard, Dusty had a foot-long Taras Bulba scalplock, while Frank brought up the rear with his shoulder-length hair, which he had chosen, in honor of the occasion, to accent with long feather earrings and a bushy fur coat that looked like he had taken it off a wolverine, *mano a mano*. I wondered if some of the Indians thought they had found a long-lost kinsman.

As ZZ took the stage for the show, I could see the members of the opening act in the front row elbowing each other and whispering. They just knew that it was only a matter of seconds before the "ZZ Tops" would make total fools of themselves trying to play music on their "chiney new geer," and the local boys would prevail. Obviously they had not even heard of the "ZZ Tops" or listened to any songs from the first album, now just beginning to circulate.

Without offering any warning—since, judging from the way the local band had started, this was the custom hereabouts—ZZ launched into the first instrumental. If you have never had the chance to hear six 100-watt Marshall stacks with the volume turned to "earbleed" in a sheet metal quonset hut with a concrete floor, believe it when I tell you it was like nuclear fission at ground zero. Hair was blown back in the first five rows. The crowd, especially the members of the opening act, were struck amazed. Not only was this the loudest music they had ever heard, it was some of the best, live and in person.

The temporary paralysis of astonishment lasted a good fifteen seconds. Then people broke out into dances that looked like a combination of the Funky Chicken and an Indian rain dance. The whole crowd acted like they were witnessing the second coming of Geronimo. The members of the first band instantly became a cheerleading squad, whooping and hollering and generally wigging out over it all. ZZ Top had again converted fans for life. For the rest of the show the entire crowd responded with the intensity of the audience at an Elvis concert.

It could have been the perfect end to a long, stress-filled day. Except that after the show was over, somebody stole the bag that held the entire gate receipts.

Smooth bummer.

Ham tried to convince the investigating officers that if they would only cooperate and give him five minutes alone with Plays-With-Machinery, *he* would get to the bottom of the mystery. The

55

stolid representatives of Española's police force politely declined his request and the money bag was never found.

I hope that somebody in Española, New Mexico, put that "lost" money to good use. Like maybe, just maybe, buying some heaters that worked and could heat up Plays-With-Machinery's "plaize."

That's what it was like. Big shows, little shows, ethnic shows. No matter what or where the gig is, you go when you're young and hungry. And you even get paid for it—mostly.

5

RAMBLIN' AND RUMBLIN'

S omewhere along the way a band feels its inertial drive increasing. A sure first sign of change is that the small and
obscure gigs become fewer and further in between. Finally,
mercifully, they vanish from the schedule altogether. Another
sign is that the number of "opener" slots dwindles in favor of
"featured," "guest attraction," or even "headliner." Moving up the
marquee is a welcome change indeed. You get bigger dressing
rooms, more stage space, and longer playing time. It only comes
about through consistently high performance and lots of exposure, including an assortment of strange performance locations
such as those mentioned in the previous chapter. Now there is a
little more money to work with, from performers to crew. A wider
viewpoint is possible and accepted.

For ZZ Top, the transition from regional band to national
band occurred in the early 1970s. Bill Ham kept the Boys out in

the spotlight; they started composing more music and getting it into album form; and the dream of true major stardom began to seem a real possibility. It was now that the promotional needs of ZZ Top conjured up a new set of interesting encounters with situations as the ladder of success was climbed.

After Woodstock got everybody's attention in the summer of '69, it seemed like back-to-nature festivals of that type started springing up everywhere. Cosmic hippies were trying to capture that magic consciousness, and solicitous promoters were trying to capture some of those magic bucks. There was obviously money to be made from the masses of freaked-out flower children willing to part with thirty or forty bucks at a pop to buy a two- or three-day dose of sensory overload. Multi-day, multi-act, and multi-chemical celebrations were popular events for any fan to attend and any band to play. Both fans and bands usually got their money's worth out of the deal. Each one of these happenings was like buying a box lunch on the fifty-yard line of a wanton drug fest and free love Deal-a-Meal.

From all bands' business standpoint, it was extremely desirable to obtain exposure to tens of thousands of money-spending people at a whack, even if a goodly portion would be too crisped on drugs to remember who they had seen and heard. A rookie act struggling for stardom would do anything to be part of one of these musical marathons, chigger bites notwithstanding.

ZZ Top made it to an outdoor orgy of this sort in Louisana in the sweltering Aquarian summer of '71. It was called the "Celebration of Life." As it turned out, it was a waste for most of the ZZ personnel concerned. Time was wasted, money was wasted; Frank and I stayed wasted; and the heat wasted Dusty. All for a misbegotten shot at time on stage in front of a semicomatose audience somewhere in the outback of southwest Louisiana.

The festival site was on some land that was bordered by the

Atchafalaya River about fifty miles west of Baton Rouge, deep in the heart of coon ass country. Since the first album hadn't made it much east of the Sabine River, ZZ Top wasn't exactly a household word in the area; therefore we weren't actually booked for the show. ZZ went because Bill Ham thought he knew somebody who could get the band on the bill. The old Texas-smoothy routine he had pulled so many times before.

The band and crew took off for this psilocybin sock hop better equipped and supplied than a British expedition setting out to find the headwaters of the Nile. This gathering of the cosmic flock was planned to last eight days—*eight!*—so Ham had spared no expense in going the distance for the chance to squeeze into the talent lineup somewhere. Like when some overmedicated group forgot what day it was and missed their scheduled chance to perform. Ham drove the band in his car so he could bend their ears for 250 miles. My van by this time was long gone; the volume of equipment had way outgrown it. Therefore Pete and I followed Ham with the gear in a PepsiCo step van. It looked like we could deliver pizzas out of that sumbitch between gigs! We didn't have any pizzas on board, but we had just about anything else you could think of.

A big funeral-sized tent had been procured for the band and Ham to sleep in. Pete and I, bearers on this safari, were slated to bunk in the equipment truck. With all the gear out it was empty, right? So why waste money on a second tent, even pup-sized. By now we almost felt like we lived in the truck of the moment anyway, so Pete and I had our survival act together. There was plenty of food and drink in the big tent, plus a portable refrigerator, a portable electric fan, portable mattresses, and a portable generator to power all of these modern portable conveniences. One guess as to who did all the porting!

By the time the ZZ entourage arrived, the festival had already been subjected to serious legal badgering by the local constabulary. A judge had issued a restraining order to reduce the length of the festival, and the planned eight days of cosmic consciousness had been cut by half. This harassment, and the midsummer heat, was starting to unravel the whole affair. The original lineup of acts was impressive, but by the time the announcer read the long list of cancellations, the four-day musical lineup had become pathetically weak. To Ham this was perfect—it cut the odds against wangling some stage time. The ZZ bandsmen were all confident that they could get on the bill with no problem, considering the circumstances.

One of the first things I remember about arriving at the scene was that Ham had to talk his way into the place. While we were hanging loose at one of the various security checkpoints we had to clear, waiting for him to exercise his influence, we all suddenly sat up and stared. Two nubile blonde-haired young goddesses were walking *stark nekkid* right out there in front of our truck! They were headed to bathe at the edge of the river, which ran through the site green and oily under the sun. It was then that we realized for the first time that this gathering was swimsuits-optional, and that most people were exercising the no-suit option. Hallelujah! What a sight. Personally, I hadn't seen that much exposed female form in one place since someone pulled the fire alarm in the girl's locker room my junior year in high school. I knew right away that this deal was going to be worth my time.

Ham finally talked the Celebration promoter into letting the ZZ expedition make camp inside the fenced-in backstage area, so we pulled in and got set up. Jesus, Joseph, and Mary, what heat! Streaming sweat, Pete and I whipped out the tent, whipped out the refrigerator, whipped out the fan, whipped out the deluxe air mattresses and sleeping bags, and whipped out the generator to power our "portable" conveniences. In the process of all that porting, we nearly got whipped out by heat prostration. Finally all was set up and we could survey our new living arrangements like overage Boy Scouts.

The first thing that became obvious was that the rented generator was *not* the quiet type. The racket it made was like a gasoline-powered chainsaw cutting into a washtub filled with ball bearings. Before long it was the bane of all the backstage staff, many a concert-goer, and anyone else who came within a half-mile or so of ZZ's campsite during the generator's hours of operation. I'll certify that it was definitely not conducive to maintaining a solid buzz, but it maintained life.

This sucker was cranked up every morning around nine or ten for several reasons. The refrigerator had to run to preserve our food, and the fan had to run to move around the stifling, humid air. And without the fridge and the fan, hopes of preserving Dusty from the elements would have been marginal at best. Dusty is not your bronze-god type sun worshipper. He is very fair-skinned, with a complexion rivaling the White Cliffs of Dover. To keep from melting into a puddle, he sat in the shade of the tent in front of the refrigerator, its door wide open, the fan stationed in front of it sucking cool air onto his tortured body. This was his station for most of the time ZZ was on this four-day musical safari. Poor Dusty suffered more than anyone, including the parboiled nocturnal denizens of the PepsiCo truck.

When the sun finally went down in the afternoon and things cooled off a bit, Dusty would venture over to the edge of the river and splash a little water on his legs. This gave him a chance to sample a little of the river ambience, namely NEKKID WOMEN EVERYWHERE. There was more wool on display than at a cashmere sweater convention. The Dust was a little bashful, though, and never did shuck his drawers and partake of the loose atmosphere. He *did* skin down to his white clinical underwear and run around like that—a smart move on his part. Dusty could burn during a solar eclipse. Keeping on his drawers meant that he didn't run the risk of setting his pecker to peeling.

Pete was his compadre in this respect. He was so modest that he never even stripped off his blue jeans or his dungaree shirt. He just went around all day with his sleeves rolled up, soaked through with sweat. It amazed me that he could survive like that, but he did.

Billy Gibbons hung around the stage area a good part of the

time. He liked watching the other acts perform, but he was itching to show *his* stuff. When Billy wasn't around the stage he was back in the tent keeping Dusty company or making humorous recordings on a portable tape deck. He could do many different voices and sound effects, and he used these talents to record fictitious interviews with concertgoers. The skits were all hilarious and helped to break the monotony of tent-side life.

Frank and I, on the other hand, had the time of our lives. Neither of us had any qualms about dropping our laundry in the middle of a city, much less in the middle of a free love hump-a-thon, so for us this was heaven on earth. Ham repeatedly told Frank and me to stick close to the stage and be ready to play, but after a day and a half of maybes and no results, Frank and I started making the river our permanent hangout. We figured that Ham would find us fast enough if any need occurred.

The most fascinating part about exposing yourself in front of hundreds of other people who are exposing themselves in front of you is that you become virtually invisible. When everyone around you is nude, you don't stick out. Well, at least you *shouldn't* stick out. For guys that would be bad form. If we did spot some overwhelmingly fine babe, we could always make a mad dash for the river and head for waist-deep water before sportin' a full blue-steel throbber. Frank and I had to head for the high tides on a couple of occasions. After a few minutes of concealment, all would be well on the social front and we could slosh back out to join the tit parade.

Another reason it was easy to mingle at a mass nude gathering was that everyone you saw was a stranger. We probably wouldn't see these people again for the rest of our lives, so whatever we did and however we looked didn't matter. Frank and I cruised nekkid up and down the edge of the river taking it all in. Feeling totally free, coupled with all the multifarious dope we sampled, produced a maximum buzz.

The only awkward moment we had was when Frank and I ran into a girl I knew from Houston. She wasn't a sexual acquaintance; that would have made it much easier to deal with. Up to this point, our relationship had been strictly business. Now that we had stumbled into each other's nude presence, we were both just a little bit embarrassed. We were no longer "invisible."

The girl had never met Frank, so minding my manners in the glorious tradition of the Old South, I attempted an introduction.

"Frank, this is Mary. Mary, this is Frank."

Ahem.

It was totally farcical. What could he say next? He couldn't very well say, "How do you do?" or "How are you?" Those facts were pretty obvious. Replying, "Nice to see you" would have sounded wise-ass and gauche at the same time. When we finally stumbled on our way, "Hope to see you again" or "Hope to see more of you" or "Nice seeing you" wouldn't have been too suave, either. As I recall, Frank used a simple, "Hi," which was about as neutral as a nude person can be.

One day Bill Ham came down to the river to join us. He took Frank and me by surprise and we almost walked right into him while we were smoking a joint. Fortunately he was so taken in by the scenery he never saw us breaking his rules. Huffing reefer in public was a bad idea from a P.R. viewpoint, not to mention the possibility of legal intervention. But the Louisiana state troopers who were patrolling the area were so busy gawking at the mass of mammaries (and wondering if any belonged to their wives or daughters), I don't think they would have noticed or cared if someone kidnapped the Lake Pontchartrain Causeway.

Ham was also shy and didn't want to go *au naturel*, so he wore his swimsuit; but he was moving his head back and forth so fast, checking out all the feminine flesh, it looked like he was watching a doubles tennis match.

"Lookee there to yer left, boy! Now over there on yer right! Gawd day-um!"

I don't think he had ever been part of anything as open as

this, so while he had his chance he was hell-bent on getting his money's worth and making the most of the circumstances.

Frank and I tried to stay pretty straight during the day in case we had to go to work; but at night, after it became obvious that ZZ wasn't going to play, we tended to get as loose as we could. Once we smoked a pipe loaded with weed, hash, angel dust, opium, and peyote. At least, that's all we could accurately identify. Remember the state of the times now, before you get judgmental.

From then on it was a slow-moving and very colorful evening for us both. The thing I remember most vividly was seeing Ted Nugent play. He was dressed only in a fur loincloth and was screaming at the top of his lungs about the wonderful guitar note he sustained for about thirty minutes. The aura he put forth was that of a psychotic Neanderthal Man who was accidentally drop-kicked into a twentieth century rock and roll band and had a guitar stuck into his hand to take the place of his club. Ol' Ted really hasn't changed much to this day. After that, Frank and I went to great lengths that night to avoid seeing Ham. That is, when we were able to think about his rules with any concentration at all.

But Ham had other things on his mind. After three days, and despite many cancellations of known bands, ZZ had still not gotten on stage. Dusty was at the limit of his heat index, and I think Pete was with him on that one. Billy was at the end of his patience and comedic tape routines. He wanted to play and was frustrated because he wasn't being allowed to. Ham was tired of trying to talk his way onto the bill and being turned down. Frank and I would have stayed the limit, but realistically we had maxed out and needed to get back to work so we could recover from the recreation.

The "Celebration of Life" ended without ZZ Top ever setting foot on stage. It was an experiential milestone; and it was the only time I ever saw Ham fail to pull one off.

One of the most startling things about working in rock and roll is when you finally realize that a good part of the time you're only moments away from violent death. While driving from show to show, the risk of winding up being extracted by the "jaws of life" from the wreckage of a grinding collision, naturally increases in direct proportion to the amount of time traveled and the number of miles put behind you. In the case of the ZZ Top crew, we traveled as much as 50,000 miles and 250 days a year or more in the early years and rarely had the luxury of a rested driver. This increased the odds of accidents or mayhem appreciably.

The same goes for airline travel. More flying time means more seduction of that temptress, Fate. In later years the band flew constantly. Dusty was intimidated by flying and would have greatly preferred to travel by bus, which they tried a few times, but Billy and Frank liked to get to the next stop as fast as possible. At one point they rented a private plane in order to circumvent the hassles of meeting commercial airline schedules, but that too was eventually scratched, partly because of the exorbitant cost and partly because of a few close calls with wind shears on takeoffs and landings.

From an equipment standpoint, band and crew were mere inches from thousands of watts of electricity and instant incineration. If ZZ was doing an outdoor show, Mother Nature would often intervene with wind or rain. Water and electricity don't mix, and wind could blow the thirty-five tons or so of steel scaffolding down on top of you and impale your ass with an X-brace. If ZZ was doing a normal inside show, there still were thousands of pounds of sound and lighting equipment hanging overhead that could drop at any time.

Suspending lighting and sound systems is down to an exact science and fairly routine, but mistakes and miscalculations can happen. ZZ had part of a sound system drop once, but luckily it was after the show was over and the crowd was gone. Like the maintenance of airplanes, great care is taken with the rigging of sound and lighting at a concert. Also like with airplanes, rigging is not *supposed* to drop to the ground, but it has before and it will again.

The most volatile ingredient of a rock concert is the crowd. This is because you can never be certain of its chemical components, socially or pharmacologically. Most of the people who came to ZZ Top shows were stoned on *something* and therefore thinking in a less-than-rational manner. I can remember a crowd pushing forward with so much intensity and mass, the stage buckled up right in the middle of ZZ's show. The remainder of the performance had to be played with a two-foot hump in the middle of the stage. Billy and Dusty just adapted and used it like it was part of the set. There wasn't a whole lot of choice.

Fatalities could occur even before the crowd got inside the venue. One year several fans were trampled and killed at a Who concert in Cincinnati by people who were rushing in to get good seats. This was partially attributable to the facility manager and promoter who tried to cut a few budgetary corners and had only opened two or three gates to save money on staff. Even greed can put you in jeopardy at a concert.

It just so happened that ZZ was the first rock act to play Cincinnati after this tragedy occurred. The city fathers had taken steps to prevent any recurrence of the Who stampede. There was more security than at the Arab/Israeli peace talks. They arranged for all the gates to be opened, and for a full staff of ticket-takers and ushers to be on hand when they were. They also had ZZ agree to let the doors open at *4:30* in the afternoon. This was highly unusual because of the setup time for shows, and the fact that all the acts involved usually did a sound check before the crowd was allowed inside. The normal time for the doors to open is an hour to an hour and a half prior to a show.

I'll always remember going to the front of the Cincinnati arena to check out the impact of this safety overkill. The only thing that even resembled a potential stampede at 4:30 in the afternoon was the security staff and four or five local "Eyewitness" news teams. They were running around photographing each other, trying to find something newsworthy. A couple of them almost knocked down some kids. I envisioned the news flash: "Concertgoers trampled by frantic reporters! Bands horrified at sight! Film at eleven!" Anything to jack up the ratings.

Death could also come instantly at the hands of some freaked-out concert party animal. I've been threatened point blank by a knife-wielding acidhead who wanted to go onstage and play with the group. Pissed-off fans, who for some reason didn't get inside to see the show because it was sold out, have cut the brake lines to our equipment trucks. Attempting to kill a truck driver was their little way of voicing disapproval with an indifferent world.

Bomb scares are nothing new, either. ZZ did a couple of shows where the decision had to be made as to whether or not the threat was serious. We were setting up for a sold-out show in Fayetteville, North Carolina, better known as "Fayette-Nam" because of the Army base there, when a police detective dropped the news on me that someone had called in a bomb threat. Because of the intense nature of the soldiers who comprised most of the potential audience, he felt it wasn't a fake.

"Somebody done got pissed off and decided if they couldn't git a ticket, then they wasn't gonna *be* no show," he explained eloquently. There were explosives on the base, and ". . . them boys is trained to use 'em." It wasn't a decision I wanted to make, but since Ham wasn't at this show, and Pete would be arriving late with the band, the ultimate responsibility for canceling or continuing was mine. It came down to choosing between potential death or guaranteed money. Since I had been educated at the Bill Ham Academy of the Entertainment Bidness, I naturally chose the guaranteed money.

When ZZ arrived just prior to showtime, I apprised the Boys of the situation. A complete search inside and out with bomb-sniffing dogs had turned up nothing, but there were no guarantees. Since Billy, Dusty, and Frank had gotten their degrees at the same school as I had, the show went on, although they did look a little edgy during their performance. You never could be sure how many of those dogs had canine sinus blockage. Fortunately, there was no bomb. Anyway, if there was one, it never went off.

During an outdoor show in Charlotte, North Carolina, a tower spotlight operator called over his headset for security. He wanted help for the guard who had been stationed at the base of the tower to prevent any of the audience from climbing on it. Then he called back. "Forget the security," he shouted. "Send a doctor and an ambulance. I think they done broke his neck!" It turned out that the guard was indeed dead, killed at the hands of so-called "fans" who wanted a better view and had become irate when the poor guy simply tried to do his job.

The most uncontrollable situations occur when the entire crowd freaks out in unison. This happened to ZZ once at an out-door show in Ithaca, New York, in 1972, where the band was the opening act for Deep Purple.

The first problem with this show was the fact that it was outdoors at a stadium that had just installed new Astroturf, and the powers that be did *not* like the idea of a crowd standing on it. I was going to find out in later years that this situation was not unique. In addition, the stage was set up to play to the *width* of the field, a headache for us because of the lack of proper access for our equipment. But to top things off, the facility manager and the promoter elected not to cover the turf. Instead, they decided they would simply use a few security guards to keep the concert-goers in the stands—on the other side of the field. Imagine putting a fifty-yard gulf between the stage and the front row of the audience. You're a kid; you brag to your friends that you have front-row tickets; then, when you get there, you find out that the front row is so far away from the stage that Bob Uecker is sitting in *front* of you! Imagine having to use binoculars to see the concert from the front row. Imagine a handful of security guards trying to keep 20,000 people in their seats fifty yards away after the first note is struck.

The whole situation was ludicrous and unimaginable, but it was actually happening. One of life's little reality checks.

When ZZ hit the first note of their set, it announced the beginning of The Great Ithaca Mass-a-Cree. Twenty thousand college kids came storming onto that field like starving army ants overrunning a South American rain forest. The fifty-yard gulf disappeared in seconds, and leading the charge were the terrified, wild-eyed security guards running like they had been set upon by hounds from Hell. Since no normal stage barricades had been erected, the front of the stage became the new front row.

Sounds exciting, right? How about adding a thunderstorm to this scenario? It had been misting before the show, so ZZ prepared by lacing up the old tennis shoes, not worn since the Fats Domino show. Onstage this would minimize the risk of electrocution; the operative word being *minimize*. But by the time the Boys finished their opening tune, the mist had transformed into a torrential downpour. The stage was half an inch deep in water and the water was rising.

Billy, Dusty, and Frank were troupers, though, and decided to give the people a little more for their money. They played two more songs and finished in the rain what had to be the most abbreviated set in ZZ history: "Thunderbird," "Beer Drinkers and Hell Raisers," and "La Grange." As all ZZ Top fans know, these are powerful and up-tempo songs which laud the merits of getting high and raising hell, not exactly the best advice to lay on twenty thousand wet, exasperated, and wired kids.

The crowd understood why ZZ had to leave the stage after so short a time, happily for us. They remained pumped up when the promoter announced over the sound system that if they would wait for the rain to stop, Deep Purple would play. This good news kept the kids at peak excitement, but it also became the third and final problem of the evening: Deep Purple had decided not to play in the rain and had left the stadium.

This was cause for serious road-crew paranoia. Over twenty thousand fans were whipped into a frenzy and had been guaranteed a show, yet now the headline act was gone. It was obvious that their highs were geared for more than three measly songs from a support act, no matter how good they had been.

When it became clear to their crew that the band was really gone, Simon, Deep Purple's sound engineer, disconnected the mixing console that was located out in the crowd. He tried *casually* to move it to the stage. But these college students were no dummies, and some of them began to inquire as to what the hell was going on. Simon told them that he was, ". . . ahhh, moving the sound mixer out of the rain. Yeaaah, that's it! The rain!" This pacified them . . . temporarily.

But when a few other party monsters in the front row noticed that the band gear and stage lighting were also being dismantled and packed, the mass-a-cree was on. The stage was attacked and overrun with irate fans hell-bent on destruction. Pete and I had managed to get all of ZZ's gear off the stage and packed during the pseudo-intermission. We had to drag speaker cabinets and drum cases to our truck in a series of mad hundred-yard dashes, but we made it. The Deep Purple crew was not so lucky. At first they armed themselves with microphone stands and attempted to hold the crowd at bay. But ten or so crew guys against an enraged army of fans were odds that were insurmountable. Rather than be torn limb from limb, the crew fell back from the front of the stage and speechlessly watched what happened next.

Deep Purple's equipment was annihilated. The first things to go were the drums, because they were the lightest objects and the most available. They were thrown off the eight-foot-high stage to the furious mob below, which immediately stomped them to pieces. The speaker cabinets and amplifiers went next, shattering as they hit the ground. Meanwhile, assault troops who had taken the stage were in the process of tearing down the lighting rig. They crushed and broke each individual fixture and bulb, no small task, since there were about 350 or 400 of them. Finally they went for John Lord's keyboard setup. The main part of this rig was a specially made Hammond organ that weighed several hundred pounds. As they pushed it toward the front of the stage, I found that I was secretly rooting for the fans. I had never seen an organ dropped from eight feet before, and I was curious what it would sound like when it hit the ground. Oddly enough, the wet turf cushioned the impact. As the organ split in half, it produced a sound something like a large mule turd hitting a boggy mire. Make that a T-Rex turd.

It was all over in just a few minutes, mainly because there was nothing left to destroy. The stage was littered with smoldering wreckage from the riot. Members of the Deep Purple crew stood around with vacant looks on their faces, like the banjo player in *Deliverance*. The angry mob disbanded, and the mass-a-cree was over.

Many an equipment scalp had been taken, but fortunately no human lives were lost. This time. Incidents like this made you wonder if rock and roll was worth it at fifteen dollars a show, my princely wage at the time. It all goes to show that there was only one reason any of us were there. We loved it.

6

RESTRICTIONS

When Ricky Staffacher (the original ZZ Top roadie) moved on in 1970, Ham promoted Pete Tickle to "equipment manager." This was quite a step up for Pete; the change in his status was as important to him as if he had been appointed to a cabinet post. I got promoted, too, from informal (if regular) associate and truck driver to "equipment technician." Hot damn! Now I was really a part of things. The former beach bum was on his way up.

I surveyed a rosy future. The band's music was great and getting better. There was no question that I enjoyed being a part of "show bidness." And of course, Bill Ham's visionary descriptions of what the future held in store for us all added to the allure of my new job. This helped to offset the fact that my starting salary was *ten dollars* a show. A dollar walked a lot taller in 1970 than it does now, but still this was not a staggering amount. Nevertheless, I was young and I had simple needs, so the deal seemed reasonable.

All of us were together constantly for the next few years, and presently our social relationships became established. No matter what the group is, over time subgroups tend to form, generated by personalities, interests, accidents, and social structure.

The formal "flow chart" of ZZ Top was the standard one you would expect: Bill Ham handled all the business arrangements and miscellaneous paperwork; Billy, Frank, and Dusty wrote and performed the music; Pete and I took care of all technical matters, including staging tactics. But this was not a coat-and-tie organization by any means. A second and every bit as important set of relationships had evolved by 1973. It boiled down to two camps: Management, consisting of Bill Ham, Billy, and Pete; and Labor, consisting of Frank, Dusty, and me. Nothing was written down about this division, but it was very clearly present.

There were several things behind this social pattern. First, the foundation of ZZ Top rested upon Bill Ham's interaction with Billy Gibbons. They had started everything, and remained together through all the staffing permutations. Billy was also the single member of ZZ Top who had been at the courthouse that day when the name was formally registered. Pete's place in the management camp was less obvious, for two reasons: He was the senior roadie, both in rank and experience; and he was a long-time personal friend of Billy's. They went back at least to the time when Billy, then with the Sidewalks, and Pete, then the lead guitarist for Dr. Pendragon and the Medicine Show, played on the same bill in Houston with the Jeff Beck Group. Pete started hauling Billy's gear on a "temporary" basis after Dr. Pendragon broke up. He never managed to put another band together, so eventually he slid into being a permanent roadie for ZZ Top. As a musician in his own right, and having had a longer period of association with Ham and Billy, it was natural that he should be closer to them than to the rest of us.

Frank, Dusty, and I were the relative newcomers, as you have seen. On the musical front, Frank and Dusty had been two-thirds of the American Blues and part of the Dallas–Ft. Worth rock scene before moving down to Houston, a history that formed the basis of their relationship. As for me, it turned out that not only was I the junior man in the tribe, my tastes for raising hell and having a good time fit dead solid perfect with the Frankster's and the Dust's philosophies of life. It didn't take long for us to become close friends and running buddies. So there you have it.

The mechanics of making ZZ Top work came out like this. Bill Ham and Billy Gibbons tended to be the ones who developed "bidness strategy" for ZZ Top, although anybody else around the office could make suggestions and comments. Whether or not they were used was another matter. If the ideas were bad, they weren't given any thought. If they were good, Ham or Gibbons would forget where the idea originally came from and conveniently "think" of it himself. Once something was cooked up, Pete and I would get moving to make sure performances came off as hoped, at least from the standpoint of equipment. Billy, Frank, and Dusty were responsible for the music, which included everything from maintaining technical skills to fomenting stage personas to writing new songs.

Due to the social relationships I just described, and because Billy unarguably did most of the songwriting, intermittent friction among the band members was inevitable. It came down to three main subjects: status, credits, and money. Over the initial three or four years, Frank and Dusty sometimes felt as if they were being treated like sidemen rather than full-fledged members of the band. Discussions of these matters between Billy, Frank, and Dusty became heated on more than one occasion, and Bill Ham got mixed in for his share, too. Frank once told me that an additional source of irritation was at the contract level: Among other things, he and Dusty had a morality clause in their contracts with

Ham's production company, while Billy did not. A morality clause basically allows a manager to pull out of the deal if he determines the other party to be morally unfit. What is actually unfit is purely subjective of course. Frank and Dusty told me that they suspected that they were singled out due to their wilder lifestyles and Ham's suspicions about their drug use. Looking back, I couldn't say Bill was all that far off base, and I bet Frank and Dusty would agree. I don't know if Bill ever removed the morality clause from Frank and Dusty's contract, or if he decided to add one to Billy's. But at the time it all made for a certain lingering animosity, the sort of thing that has ruined many another musical relationship.

But in the case of ZZ Top, several forces kept the band together. For one thing, Bill Ham paid close attention to what was going on amongst his troops. He was a born leader, older and more cunning than any of us. He used whatever tool seemed right at the moment to keep it all going, ranging from promises and persuasion, to threats and pure checkbook diplomacy. Whether it was grumbling, chemical vagaries, or social indiscretions, you could count on Bill Ham to spot and fix the trouble fast.

Even if the "sideman syndrome" never disappeared entirely, the more important "credits and money situations" were rectified by Ham before they could destroy ZZ Top. "He who has more credits, gets more money"; so it is written in the music business. The stage show was never much of a problem because each musician shared equally, or nearly so. On the question of recordings, however, the first three ZZ Top albums laid out song credits according to how much each man contributed *lyrically* to a piece. This is why even Bill Ham's name appeared on several songs on the early albums; if he suggested a lyric here or there, he would usually get writer's credits. But Frank and Dusty, as integral elements in ZZ Top's sound, objected in a big way to how the record money was split up. Ham very intelligently convinced Billy to give way to save the golden goose, and after the *Tres Hombres* album, equal credits (and resulting profits) were awarded to all.

I got familiar with all the personalities in the ZZ Top circus,

75

especially with "labor," but least closely with Billy Gibbons. We had a friendly enough relationship, but Billy was always subtly distant and more difficult to get to know. Without anybody usually realizing it, Billy had a way of maintaining a careful emotional distance from people he wasn't sure he wanted to know. And he rarely, if ever, let you into his confidence.

Billy was a chameleon. He could sidestep probing questions by getting people to talk about things *they* were interested in, instead of him having to talk about himself. Billy had a broad enough range of knowledge to be completely convincing while discussing any topic, even when he was out-and-out bullshitting. For instance, if you were a fly fisherman, by God, it just so happened that he had tied a few flies himself. If you were a truck driver, then Billy would tell you about his gear-jamming days. Why, if you were an *archeologist*, he'd tell you about a few digs he'd been on! One could never be sure when Billy was being truthful, borrowing from something he'd read, or recalling someone else's experiences as if they were his own. This way, he avoided revealing much about himself; plus, he had a good time playing with people's heads, especially those of interviewers.

One "borrowed" recollection I know of for sure was Billy's story about how the idea came up for the ZZ song "Ten Foot Pole." He told the press about how he was hiking through the Himalayas and rested at a campfire with some local mountain folks. While he sat there, the natives started to chant and sing to this weird beat they were laying down on drums and gourds. They were supposedly trying to call down the Abominable Snowman. This, according to Billy, was the inspiration for the beat and lyrics of the song. Actually he had heard the Snowman story from a friend of his; embellishments were added to suit Billy's purpose. And the purpose was? Purely to see how much "snow" the press would buy.

Occasionally, this tendency of Billy's would create interesting situations during interviews. Gibbons would begin a lie in response to an interviewer's question, and then call on Frank or

Dusty to finish the story like they had been there. I'm convinced that some of the wild rumors about ZZ, like them supposedly giving half their earnings to the National Organization for the Reform of Marijuana Laws, stemmed from some of these disjointed story lines, or "Fractured Fairy Tales" if you will.

Frank and Dusty were totally different from this. What you saw was what you got with those two. There wasn't much deception to them. I guess that's why we got along as well as we did. Whatever we were, it was right there on the surface to turn around in your hands and look at; just make sure to wash your hands when you're finished.

Frank, Dusty, and I tended to avoid going down to Bill Ham's office because it held uncomfortable associations. When Ham called us in there, it was usually for a bitchout/sermon about some transgression or another we had just committed. I'll have to admit that labor raised a disproportionately larger amount of hell than management—at least we got caught more than Billy or Pete—so sometimes those sermons were deserved. When we were told to come in for a meeting with Ham, we all acted like death row inmates whose stays of execution had been revoked.

Once Frank and I were called in to Ham's office together for a bitchout/sermon about rule-breaking. You see, from time to time Ham would make rules and issue restrictions to the band members, on the notion that certain things must be done to promote and preserve ZZ Top's "image" (whatever that was). This particular summons dealt with my having helped Frank break one of the earliest Ham Commandments, "No going to clubs where you might be spotted by your public." Ham was dead serious about all public relations issues; he felt that incautious fraternization could damage the charisma of the band members he was trying to create.

We were worried enough about this particular confrontation

to feel the need for some intense preliminary chemical therapy, to the point of near catatonia. As a consequence, Frank and I showed up at the office working a very large "nod" behind some very good brown. Ham's office at that time had no windows and was fairly dark; nonetheless, we wore our opaque dark glasses and kept them on. The only light in the room came from Ham's desk lamp, pointed, à la Nazi-interrogation style, directly at us. The idea was to obscure his face from our vision, an unnecessary ploy, since both our visions had already been obscured by choice. Paying a visit to Ham was like going to see your proctologist. No, worse! His presence behind the desk was ominous, intimidating, and all-powerful.

As Ham began speaking I looked over at Frank and noticed that he was slouched down in his chair, chin on his chest, scratching his nose, and beginning to nod out. I was also failing miserably at maintaining consciousness. All I can remember was muttering a "Yeah, Bill," an "I'm sorry, Bill," and a final "I'll never do it again, Bill," complete with quivering lip and misty eyes. Frank also managed to appease Ham, his rhetoric running along the same erudite lines as mine.

After our conversation we shuffled out, heads still down. As we got outside we ran into Dusty, who was there for a similar "talk" about whatever errors in judgment *he* had committed. It was pure *deja vu*; Dusty was wearing sunglasses just like ours, and working a major chemical-therapy nod. His stuff must have been better than ours, though; he was so hammered he had his shoes on the wrong feet! Dusty was embarrassed about it later, and tried to convince Frank and me that those were specially designed jogging shoes that could be worn on either foot. You bet, Dust!

The more famous ZZ Top became, the more restrictions Ham laid down. This tightening of the leash was not accepted in a positive spirit by those affected, and it eventually evolved into a game of hide-and-seek. Frank, Dusty, and I would hide, Ham would seek. It got to be a comic opera sometimes, starring characters right out of a Marx Brothers movie.

The activity Ham decreed to be the most major taboo was the inhalation of smoke produced by burning a non-tobacco product. I have already mentioned that on occasion labor (at least) would partake of fine herbs. This rule, an immediate style-cramper for Frank and me, came down after a show ZZ did in Austin, Texas, way back in 1970.

After the gig, Frank, Pete, and I decided to go visit Billy Ethridge, the erstwhile ZZ Top bass player who was living there at the time. I should note in passing that this was *before* the rule restricting preshow and post-show movements of individual band members, about which more will be said. Though it was a rare thing for him to fraternize with the troops, Bill Ham decided to go along with us this time. If he was gathering data to make a case against after-show visits, he was not disappointed.

We were having a good time listening to Frank and Ethridge tell old war stories and swap lies. The tale I remember the most was one Frank told. He once left a large fecal specimen of his in Ethridge's cat's litterbox. When Ethridge discovered it, the dimensions of the matter horrified him. He went on a frantic search for his beloved cat, Bach, thinking the poor critter must be off somewhere hemorrhaging. Bach under his arm, he was nearly out the door heading for the vet when Frank let him in on the prank.

On the basis of such inspired humor our visit with Ethridge became very upbeat. It was natural that somebody fire up a Mexican Marlboro and begin passing it around. Frank and I didn't think twice about participating in this social exchange, quite normal for the time. I failed to notice Ham's reaction, but I did notice that Pete, who normally smoked with us, had suddenly decided to pass on his turn. I finally realized what was going on when I saw Ham squirming around in his chair like he had his underwear on backwards, and Pete looking like a man waiting for the results of a tumor biopsy. The only trouble was that by then I was too stoned to care, and took in the whole situation with an expansive and uninhibited sense of well-being.

Back in Houston the next day, and back from being more than a bubble off, I learned from Pete that Ham was furious with Frank for smoking pot in front of him. He was mad at me, too, but Frank naturally was his first concern. Since Frank and I were tight, I thought I'd better warn him about the looming thunder-cloud on the near horizon. After I did, Frank immediately called Ham up to apologize for his blatant indiscretion, thereby getting himself off the hook. By doing so, unfortunately, he unwittingly set me up for serious trouble. Frank had made the initial move to apologize, thereby depriving Ham of the element of surprise and deflating the effect of any impending bitchout/sermon. This meant that *I* was now the primary target for Ham's ire.

I got the call. "Me and you got a couple things to talk about."

By the time I walked in the door of Ham's office to take my medicine, he had decided that my warning Frank was the worst information leak since the Pentagon Papers. As I sat down, staring up into the usual blinding glare of lamplight, Ham told me point blank that I was fired.

Fired! I was stunned. My roadie career was just getting started; I had bills to pay; I . . . As I writhed, torn by all sorts of confused feelings, Ham leaned toward me and began to speak.

The sermon's theme was about the responsibility "we" had to ZZ Top, and how "we" were on the threshold of creating a major attraction, and how "we" could ruin it all if somebody got busted for dope. If "we" didn't screw it up, "we" would all eventually be set for life. In no time at all I felt lower than the Dow on Black Monday. Yep, it was all true. I'd been a bad, bad boy. "We" really did need to watch it, or else. . . .

"We?" I suddenly thought. Hey, wait a minute. "We" wasn't "me" anymore. I'd just gotten fired, for Chrissakes!

I don't know what got into me but I reared up and said something for once. I took the opportunity to observe, essentially in non sequitur, that Ham's income from ZZ Top had been increasing at a noticeably faster rate than mine. I mean, at that time Pete and I were dividing a grand total of $25 per show between us. Counting loading, setup, drive, and gig time, we were working eighteen to twenty hours per gig. When the drives were long between shows there was no sleep time built in, so for these we worked virtually twenty-four hours straight. In round figures this worked out to about one dollar an hour, and we had to split that. But not fifty-fifty, either. Since Pete was "equipment manager," he got *60* percent and I got *40* percent. Forty cents an hour, by God! Bill Ham was doing a tad better than that!

Now, whenever the issue of money was brought up, Ham would brush by it in a hurry. Like whenever Frank and Dusty got the nerve to ask to "look at the books" (which happened at least once) to see why they weren't receiving more money than they were, Ham would get his spiel into high gear. They'd walk out pacified, even elated—but usually without ever seeing the books. So I expected it when Ham said with contrived sincerity and equal irrelevance, "Lissen, boy, I put my pants on one leg at a time, just like you."

That wasn't good enough *this* time! Tracking the metaphor, I pointed out that he was stepping into Italian silk while I was stepping into patched Levi's, congratulating myself on being pretty cute as I said it. I didn't get to smirk for long. As always then or later, when Ham got cornered, he managed to come out on top simply by ignoring all sarcasm and lighting into that inspirational monologue of his.

I'll tell you what: When you heard one of the Reverend Ham's motivational sermons you forgot all about money and material possessions. Bill Ham would tell you things that got you fired up and ready to carry the ZZ flag, boy. HOT DAMN! In just a few moments I knew I really had sinned, and badly. I hung my head low at being revealed for what I really was. Of course he had to fire me. Why hadn't I seen it before?

I wish I could recall this in more detail for you. The only

trouble was, it was always hard to remember what Bill Ham had said because he usually said it with the pace and enunciation of a tobacco auctioneer. But he could tap into a person's innermost feelings and knew just which strings to pull to rekindle a dying flame. This is one of the attributes that made him a good manager. At his best, Bill Ham could make the Reverend Billy Graham look like he needed a refresher course in motivational oratory and faith.

By the time Ham finished with me, I had seen the light, realized the wickedness of my ways, and had apologized for the sins I had committed against Ham's Commandments. Upon which, appeased, Bill Ham unfired me. All right! I left his office feeling like a born-again Christian on Easter Sunday morning. I was still going to be able to work for forty cents an hour! Twenty-four hours a day! Whew! Be still my heart!

We may be fortunate that Bill Ham decided to operate in the reasonably innocuous "music bidness" instead of in politics, or from a pulpit. Lyndon Johnson or Oral Roberts would have had to eat Bill Ham's dust.

Another offense that Ham soon decreed as grounds for termination was "swiggin' while giggin'." The no-alcohol-before-a-show restriction didn't rain on Billy's parade one bit because he was into transcendental meditation by this time and could get his pre-show jollies by meditating in the dressing room, tuned in to the Maharishi's wavelength. Frank and Dusty were cut from a different cloth. They were raised in clubs playing six sets a night and drinking seven. Both were accustomed to partaking of the grape just prior to doing a show. They felt like it helped to bolster a feller's spirits if done in moderation.

Of course, Frank hadn't practiced moderation since Moby Dick was a minnow. It was mainly a gigantic *faux pas* of his that brought down solid enforcement of Bill Ham's Third Commandment. This incident came in the period just after the No-Alcohol Rule but before the Restricted-Travel-of-the-Band-Members-on-Show-Day Rule.

We had a show lined up at Armadillo World Headquarters in Austin, in the 70s one of the premier venues in the state of Texas. As you may have suspected from the vapor-therapy story, Frank always seemed to get into trouble in Austin, like he was influenced by evil demons, or maybe Communist thought-control. Since ZZ got into town a little early, he decided to go "visit some old friends for a little while." Unfortunately, "a little while" turned out to be all day.

By the time the opening act at Armadillo World Headquarters had started to play, Ham was worried but cool. By the time the opener finished and Frank still hadn't shown, Ham was noticeably agitated. During the second act some people might have described him as freaking out. Where in the hell was Frank? Had anybody seen him? Damn it, this bidness was enough to swell your hemorrhoids!

Finally, a few short minutes before ZZ was due on stage, Frank showed up. Ham's worst premonitions were justified: Frank was in the middle stages of a knee-walking drunk, as was most of his associated entourage, one of whom was none other than Billy Ethridge, the demon seed of that other fateful night! Frank calmly slurred the explanation to Ham that everything was cool and that he could play "jist fine." Heck, he'd just been teaching his pals a new beer-drinking technique he had recently learned called shot-gunning. This involved opening a hole in the side of a beer can near the bottom edge, putting your mouth over the hole, and then turning it right side up as you popped open the regular tab. Gravity caused the beer to gush out in an unstoppable stream, and you had the choice of either sucking it right down or wearing it.

From the looks of things, Frank had been exercising both options quite extensively. Naturally he had made it an afternoon-long contest between his buddies and himself, and I remember him saying it had gotten tied up at around a dozen apiece before someone remembered that Frank had to play a gig. Frank was in rare form for this one.

Ham made a hurried attempt to find someone to sit in on drums for Frank but naturally no one could because you sorta have to know the material. Finally there was no choice; it was show time. No play, no pay. No pay? After carefully weighing his options and reviewing the lesson plan of the Bill Ham Academy of the Entertainment Bidness, Ham sent Frank out with the others.

The crowd got their money's worth that night. When it got down to the last song in the set, "Brown Sugar," it was time for each band member to do a solo. Dusty did his bass solo and Frank somehow managed to pull off his drum solo. He had been struggling just to play throughout the whole show, but his automatic pilot mode was pretty good, so he managed to fake it. But by the time he finished his solo, he was wasted.

Now it was Billy's turn to blow, a solo that lasted five minutes or so. Frank decided to take an extemporaneous if much needed break. He wobbled away from his drums and began wandering around the stage area, front and back. It was like he was taking a meandering Sunday stroll through the middle of the show. Billy ignored him and just kept on playing. All of a sudden, Frank emerged from behind Billy's speaker stacks wielding a cymbal stand like a Samurai sword. He approached Gibbons with a maniacal grin on his face and said, "I'm gonna smash your fucking guitar!" Billy calmly continued to play, tilted his head back, smiled a smile that the Maharishi himself would have envied, and said, "Naw, man, don't do that."

By this time Ham feared that the situation was reaching critical mass. Creeping out on stage, and failing miserably at trying not to be noticed by the audience, he positioned himself behind Billy's speaker stacks. Before Frank could take a swipe at Billy's classic Les Paul guitar, Miss Pearly Gates, Ham stuck his head out from behind the stacks and yelled, "Frank! You've gone too far this time!" Frank looked blearily at Ham and smirked, halting his

1965
Billy Gibbons (*left*), Mike Frazier (*center*), Bob Braden (*right*), Dan
Mitchell (*drums*), and Cindy Sexias (*go-go girl*). The Coachmen play at a
car trade show, in eye-catching coordinates. *(Dan Mitchell Archives)*

1965
Billy Gibbons and the Coachmen. Young Christians go mod for God.
(Dan Mitchell Archives)

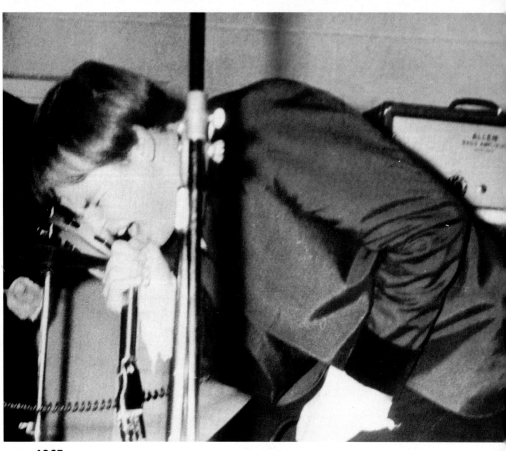

1965
Billy Gibbons sings James Brown during a Coachmen gig—*owwwwww!*
(Dan Mitchell Archives)

1966
Robert E. Lee High, Houston, Texas. Billy Gibbons in his junior year.

1966–67
Don Summers, Mike Moore, Dan Mitchell, Billy Gibbons. "Mod" Moving
Sidewalks promo picture. Look out Dave Clark Five! *(Dan Mitchell
Archives)*

1968
Jimi Hendrix with the Moving Sidewalks. *(Dan Mitchell Archives)*

1968
Dan Mitchell, Mike Moore, Don Summers, Billy Gibbons. The Moving Sidewalks—longer hair, meaner looks. *(Dan Mitchell Archives)*

196195

JUN-20-69 B 51 8 4 0   NA196195 D — — PD$$$2.0
JUN-20-69 B 51 8 4 1   NA196195 D — — PD$$$1.

OFFICE OF
R. E. TURRENTINE, JR.
COUNTY CLERK
HARRIS COUNTY
HOUSTON, TEXAS

June 20, 1969

ADDRESS ALL CORRESPONDENCE TO
P. O. BOX 1525
HOUSTON, TEXAS 77001

This is to acknowledge receipt of Certificate of Operation under Assumed Name which was
filed in my office for ___Z.Z. TOP___ 602 Westbury Sq.
Houston, Texas ___,
under File Number as shown on cash register validation above, and indexed in Record of Persons
Operating under Assumed Name as prescribed by law. The Certificate shows

Dan M Mitchell , Bill Gibbons and Lanier H. Greig,Jr.

to be the owner_s_ of said business. The above described Certificate is valid for a period of 10
years from the date it was filed; after which it will be null and void unless renewed prior to its
expiration date.

Whenever there is a change of ownership of any business operating under any such assumed
name, the person or persons withdrawing from said business or disposing of their interest there-
in, shall file in the office of the clerk of the county in which such business is being conducted
and has a place or places of business, a certificate setting forth the fact of such withdrawal
from or disposition of interest in such business; and until he has filed such certificate he shall
remain liable for all debts incurred in the operation of said business.

A Withdrawal Certificate shall be executed and duly acknowledged by the person or persons
so withdrawing from or selling their interest in said business in the manner now provided for
acknowledgment of conveyance of property.

Yours very truly,

R. E. Turrentine, Jr.,
County Clerk, Harris County

By _____ Florence Campbell _____
Deputy

Form No. CC-B-03-13-07 (R-10/8/62)

June 20, 1969
The original document registering ZZ Top's name. *(Dan Mitchell Archives)*

Fall 1969
ZZ Top (version 2): Billy Gibbons, Dan Mitchell, Billy Ethridge.
(Dan Mitchell Archives)

Circa 1972
Billy and Pearly, a love
affair. *(Paul Seward)*

Circa 1972
Beardless Billy strains to
emote and hit a note.
(Paul Seward)

Circa 1972
Billy and Pearly Gates get nasty. *(Paul Seward)*

Circa 1975
Lounging on the steps of the original Chicken Ranch in LaGrange, which was the basis for *The Best Little Whorehouse in Texas.* *(Galen Scott)*

course toward Billy. Slowly it registered that he was being scolded. Whoa! We don't want *that*! Gotta get rid of this thing I'm holdin'!

He launched the cymbal stand like a hammer thrower. It disappeared over the top of the speaker stacks and into the darkness of backstage, landing with a crash. The stand didn't hit anyone, but unfortunately it barely missed hitting Billy Ethridge. He and the rest of Frank's gang were sitting backstage and still shotgunning beers. The reason I say "unfortunately" is because Ethridge perceived the intrusion of a flying cymbol stand as a direct affront. He didn't hesitate to grab it and immediately hurl it back in the general direction it had come from. His hand-eye coordination, more than slightly dulled from shotgunning a dozen or so beers, caused him to miss his mark, which was Frank, and land only a few feet from an agreeable secondary target, which was Ham.

Imagine the picture: Gibbons trying to play, Frank wandering aimlessly about the stage, Ham frantically trying to talk sense into him while dodging flying cymbal stands and trying futilely to hide from the audience. Meanwhile, Dusty just stood on his side of the stage and took it all in. He knew better than to get involved.

Billy finally approached the end of his solo. Frank heard his cue coming and weaved back to his drums. Still flying on auto pilot, he came in on beat perfectly and finished the tune like nothing had happened. The audience began cheering and applauding while Ham tried unsuccessfully to duck-walk offstage without being seen. Meanwhile, Ethridge and party kept shotgunning beers. As quickly as it had erupted, the chaos vanished into the haze and daze of Armadillo World Headquarters. I never did find out who won the shotgunning contest.

You can see why it was not long after this that Ham's commandment about boozing before playing was joined by one prohibiting unsupervised preshow visitation. I might add that Ethridge assumed total pariah status as far as Bill Ham was concerned, but you've probably guessed that by now.

The restrictions Ham placed on the group were supposed to be constantly in effect. As mentioned before, when the band was in Houston, all clubs and bars that might be frequented by ZZ Top fans were deemed off-limits. That pretty much covered every good spot in town. Sometimes the roadies went to a lot of trouble to help the band members sneak around, even though the crew was supposed to monitor band member movements and report any rule infractions back to headquarters. It's hard to believe that Ham really expected us to rat on the guys and still be able to maintain a smooth-working relationship with them, but he did.

One night Frank *had* to go see Emmy Lou Harris at a Houston club called Liberty Hall. She was playing there with Commander Cody and the Lost Planet Airmen (there's another great package for you!). We had two additional crew members at the time, Dave "Grizz" Rowe (who had more body hair than an alpaca) and Randy "Lit Joint" Fletcher (who always smelled like a lit joint and had the biggest smile this side of Little Richard's piano keys). The three of us sandwiched Frank in between us, had him wear a floppy hat, and covered his face with some dark glasses. Sporting this disguise, we eased him through the front door of Liberty Hall and up to refuge in the dark balcony. Safe!

Frank remained incognito the entire night by sitting in the darkest corner of the club. If he had to go to the bathroom, he went sandwiched between us. If he wanted something to drink, one of us went and got it. Great pains were taken to ensure that Frank wasn't discovered, because word was sure to get back to Ham if he was.

At the end of her show, which had been great as ever, Frank wanted to meet Emmy Lou, so I was elected to go to her dressing room to arrange it. I talked my way backstage using ZZ's name and located Emmy Lou with little difficulty. I explained that the drummer from a local band wanted to meet her but he couldn't come backstage because he couldn't be seen. Wondering what was up, Emmy Lou asked which band. When I told her she smiled and agreed to come with me. I escorted the friendly and hospitable Miss Harris to the balcony and introduced her to Frank. They talked for a few minutes about nothing in particular, then Emmy Lou made her farewells and went back to her dressing room. Frank, his ambition for the evening having been achieved, was ready to leave. We sandwiched him between us for the final time and escorted him out of the club into the relative safety of the night. On the way home Frank was breaking his arm patting himself on the back for accomplishing this bit of rock and roll subterfuge.

The next day we found out that Ham wanted to break some arms himself. Somehow he had gotten wind that Frank was out "clubbing" the night before. To make matters worse, Ham knew he was out with *us*. To set an example for the rest of the crew, he fired me! Again! My rock and roll train had derailed a second time.

I was finally called into Ham's office a few days later, and after letting fly with a proper bitchout/sermon and hearing my apology, he agreed to rehire me. But it cost me a $25-a-week cut in my already anemic salary, which recently had been upped to $150 a week. Just like the time before, Ham's rhetoric was so majestic that it seemed a small price to pay to re-enlist in ZZ Top's rock and roll army.

Of course, Gibbons went to clubs while he was in Houston, too, but he approached it a little more circumspectly. He would go to a Black club called Miss Irene's, usually alone. Billy would even get on stage with different bands that played there and jam with them, only instead of playing guitar he played harmonica. The shirt he sometimes wore had a picture of a harmonica embroidered on the back, along with the name "Mellow Larry." The fans in the club got to the point where they actually requested him by name, yelling out, "Let Mella' Larry play." Sometimes the best cover is either no cover at all, or a ridiculous one. Billy never got caught, so I guess he knew what he was doing.

Frank continued trying to find loopholes in the restrictions. For example, he figured that all bets were off if ZZ crossed an international border. That's how he tried to justify a drunk we threw in Mexico one night.

ZZ had done a show in McAllen, Texas. Since it was a border town, the standard procedure was for Ham to take the band across into Mexico for a good time. Ham and Gibbons loved Mexico and would rarely pass up an opportunity to go there for the food, overall atmosphere, and "field research" for future use. Frank, Dusty, and I went for the less esoteric reasons of cheap cigarettes and cheap booze.

What made this trip a little different from the usual was that we were escorted by a guy named Joe who lived in McAllen but worked across the border for the city of Reynosa. Ham had obtained Joe's services, such as they were, as a guide and gofer. I don't know where he ran across this dude, but his appearance and background were what you could call sketchy. The Mexicans referred to him as El Gringo Peligroso, which translates roughly as "the bad-news American." For those of you who are curious, there's a picture of Joe on the liner sleeve of ZZ's *Tres Hombres* album. He's the guy with the wild eyes holding a machine gun and standing next to his pickup truck, with two other automatic weapons on the hood. Case closed. Just the sort of assistant you need when you take a stroll south of the border.

When we arrived at the Rio Grande, the Mexican guards eyeballed all the long hair and decided we couldn't cross. It seems they were cracking down on hippie drug smugglers at the time. Joe started giving them a ration of shit in rapid-fire Mexican street lingo. He told them that ZZ was part of a government cultural exchange program and that a Mexican rock band was playing on the U.S. side while ZZ was going over to play on the Mexican side. Since he spoke Spanish like a native, had papers saying he worked for the city of Reynosa, and was a serious bad-looking gringo, the border guards decided they would be well-advised not to detain this dude or anybody associated with him. We proceeded to "exchange" our asses across the border.

Every border town has a section referred to as Boy's Town. This is where all the hot clubs are located, and in nature's scheme of things this is where the rentable *señoritas* display their wares. Many a small-town Texas boy has gone to one of these red-light districts for his first drunk and/or to lay his first pipe, before later growing up to be a distinguished congressman or senator.

We headed straight for a club Joe knew of that had a live band. This turned out to be one of those rare occasions when Ham let ZZ sit in and jam. He always loosened up on this policy in Mexico. I guess Ham figured the Boys couldn't "damage their charisma" in Mexico. So during a break, ZZ played a few songs on the house band's funky little instrument setup.

No matter how cheap the equipment, Billy, Dusty, and Frank were always able to make it sound like it just came off the showroom floor. Hearing them play without their own equipment and effects, I could appreciate all the more their individual talents and contributions to the overall ZZ Top style and sound. There was an obvious musical chemistry between them. During one of the "management" *vs.* "labor" disputes, Dusty and Frank told me confidentially that the only time they could stand to be around Billy was the two hours or so they were on stage; but for that length of time they were in *love* with him. Hearing ZZ in the Mexican club made me reflect on the components of their music and how it had developed to that point.

When it comes to breaking their sound into parts, Frank is the meter man—"the human metronome." Even though his drumming sometimes comes out a bit slushy, his tempo dynamics are a major ingredient of the ZZ sound and feel. If everything he played was to exact meter, the texture of the music would be too rigid. Slop can make you bop, I guess you'd say.

Dusty carries the bottom end. Ol' Thumper. He can play a lot more bass guitar than Billy's prerequisites allow him to show. Gibbons would just say, "Lay down the bed and I'll play on top of it." This sometimes frustrated Dusty, because he would have liked to play more intricate material. Dusty was never satisfied with the number of vocals he did on the albums, either. He was the front man for every other group he had been a part of and never got accustomed to playing a secondary vocal role. In live presentations, Dusty got to sing more and he also played a big part in the unique choreography ZZ developed.

Without a doubt, Billy remains ZZ Top's focal point. It's his presence for which ZZ is most known, and his guitar playing ability remains the band's biggest asset. Known guitar players like Jeff Beck, Duane Allman, Eddie Van Halen, Eric Johnson, and others have greatly admired his styling in live presentations as well as in the studio. He has a wonderful ability to intertwine lead and rhythm parts simultaneously during live shows. The three-piece format is the hardest for a guitar player to pull off. If you play three-piece, you had better have your chops together. Billy Gibbons *has* his chops together.

Billy also provides most of the vocals. Although he would not be classed as a singer *per se*, he is definitely a vocal stylist. His comic nature enhances the delivery of the lyrics. This humor bubbling away under the surface of ZZ's music is a big reason for the band's vast popularity. Plain and simple, the Boys are fun to see and fun to listen to.

A club-jam situation like this one in Mexico was the definitive way to see the three Boys interact. Next to private rehearsals, it was the best environment in which to hear ZZ. They were being totally genuine. They all had plenty of leeway to loosen up and play the way they really wanted. Dusty would take over as the front man and do most of the singing and talking. It was obvious that he felt more at home in a club situation. He would pull out all his old lounge jokes and routines and really shine. Frank was free to sit back and play funky drums without having to worry about perfect time. Sometimes he had more fun paying attention to what was going on around him than onstage. He could hold entire conversations with people while he was playing. If he was off a little or missed a cue, fuck it. This arrangement suited Billy just fine as well. It freed him to do nothing but play guitar, which is what he does best. Not having to sing while he played made a big difference in his overall delivery.

After ZZ finished sitting in at the Mexican club we called it an evening and headed back towards the good ol' U.S. of A. Ham, Gibbons, and Tickle went one way as usual, and Joe guided Frank, Dusty, and me the other—the old management/labor split revealing itself again. Labor stopped off along the way to buy some booze at Mexican prices (you just can't turn 'em down), and somewhere around three in the morning we made it back to the bridge over the Rio Grande.

As we came up to the bridge, Frank and I were sitting in the backseat of the car having a straight likker chug-a-lug contest—one of Frank's more inspired ideas. We each turned a quart straight up; the one who stopped drinking first would be the loser. Nothing but egos were on the line, but those were high stakes to us. Joe and Dusty watched it all in amusement from the safe vantage point of the front seat.

After what seemed like an eternity of liquid flame, the back of my throat was hotter than a fresh-fucked fox from a flamin' forest fire. I just had to lower my bottle and admit defeat. But look! There was Frank, lowering *his* bottle at the same time. Tie! Frank measured what was left of our bottles' contents, and after close inspection with his razor-sharp micro-sensitive eyesight determined them to be equal. Tie again!

Naturally this required a tie-breaker. Southern duels are not over until blood has been drawn or victory acknowledged. Since by this time we had to pee in the worst way, Frank decided a peeing contest would be the perfect way to settle who the best man was. The one who finished first would be declared the loser. He looked out the window and saw that we were approaching the crown of the international bridge. "Stop the car!" he yelled. Frank

91

designated dead center of the Rio Grande as the perfect peeing contest site. Intellects honed to maximum acuity by a combined half-gallon of whiskey reasoned that if they hold Super Bowls in super domes, a super peeing contest should be held over such an important body of water. Also, peeing from the center of the Mexican-American border would create a spirit of international fair play and help maintain contest neutrality. We were drunker than a Tailhook convention by this time, and the thought that we might simultaneously be breaking the obscenity laws of two governments never even occurred to us.

We whipped out our hoots and did our business. Joe and Dusty took the lookout for *federales* as casual observers. I finished first—damn it!—and was declared the loser. I had even tried to get an edge by pinching off every so often to prolong endurance and lengthen my pee elapsed time, but it didn't work. Frank must have a bladder the size of a beach ball, because he beat me by a good fifteen or twenty seconds. It was too late by then, but I dimly recalled that on trips every time we stopped to pee by the roadside Frank would have enough staying power to write his first, middle, and last name, dot everybody else's *i*'s, and write one or two amendments to the Constitution. Frank could outpiss a plow mule, so I never had a chance.

Through the fog of night Joe got us back to the apartment where we were staying. As we pulled up, Frank noticed some underwear hanging on a nearby clothesline. This required analysis, and a huddle. Inside the apartment, we decided that the garments must belong to some girls.

GIRLS, the man said? *Panocha?* I'm there, dude!

We wanted to hotfoot it out the door in search of these imaginary sirens, but by this time our hot feet weren't working too hot. Since walking was out of the question, this left us no option but to crawl next door on our hands and knees. Frank and I probably figured at the time (using our powers of geometric thinking) that no one would notice. We were at the door, merrily crawling our way out with me in the lead but Frank in hot crawl pursuit, when I ran into a pair of kneecaps. I slowly raised my eyes. There was the *knee*bone, next the *thigh*bone; and there was the *hip*bone. I focussed upward with some difficulty past all the rest of the bones.

It was . . . the *Ham*bone!

"You boys goin' somewhere?" Bill Ham asked, grinning.

I remember seeing Frank look sheepish, regarding Ham from his four-point full-race crawl position, moving his mouth but forming no words. I tried to help, babbling weakly. If the world would just stop spinning around so unhelpfully I could explain. No luck. The last thing I remember is the ground rushing up to hit me between the eyes.

The next day was pure hell. Frank said he felt like he'd been shot at and missed and shit at and hit. Aside from the artillery practice they were holding inside my skull, my throat felt like I had gargled with napalm and rinsed with Drano. Frank and I had relearned in depth the meaning of the expression "a knee-walking drunk."

Yessir. We had all gotten to know each other *real* well by the end of 1973. Bill Ham more than anybody. He knew everybody's strengths and weaknesses, and through exercise of the Commandments and as much enforcement as he could muster, the gigs rolled along, getting bigger and bigger. And we rolled along with them.

7

ROAD WARRIORS

During the early 1970s, ZZ Top and a lot of other Southern bands took to the highways and began "power touring" all over the United States. This was not for love of life on the road. No indeed! We all went out there for a very good reason, one dictated by simple economics. You had to maintain that old exposure to survive.

In the music business, money is generated through concerts and through the sale of recordings. Tapes and CD's provide the lion's share of profits because they're less expensive per unit and last awhile, meaning that people tend to put more money into recordings overall than they do into concerts. Ironically, however, recordings for the most part don't sell well enough without live concerts to back them up. The reason is very simple: A band eventually needs to put its face on the case.

There are tens of thousands of excellent musicians, thousands of excellent bands, and hundreds of bands peddling record albums. The music fan who walks into any record store immediately overdosed on choices. So if you want Joe High School or Jolene College to slap down some fun tickets for one of *your* group's albums, you'd better have already made an impression on them beforehand, and a good one. You need that *exposure* so they'll remember you. In case there's any doubt about it in any reader's mind, this is also why musicians dress the way they do. They want you to remember them when you go out to get that album.

Believe it or not, once upon a time in America there was no MTV. That's right, none at all. So a band couldn't reach the fans through television, unless it got super lucky and landed a shot on something like "Saturday Night Live" or "American Bandstand." Even "Austin City Limits" didn't start up broadcasts until 1975. Radio, then as now, was a pretty iffy proposition; you just couldn't depend on those flakey DJ's to play your stuff. They were too busy dreaming up unique radio promotions like "Win ZZ Top for a Day." This was a serious problem for Southern rock groups, unlike those based on either coast—all of the major urbanized belts were right in the backyards of the California and neo-Brit bands. To tap into these lucrative market areas, the Southerners had to charge and take things by storm.

This meant touring—forever. Or so it seemed to us at the time.

In the early half of the 1970s, the highways were so jammed with band tour buses and equipment trucks that the roads looked like day-old pizza overrun by crazed, starving cockroaches. The ZZ crew would almost always see another band or road crew at each truck stop where a break was taken. This would provide scintillating conversation and the swapping of critical information between technicians.

"You played there?"

"Yeah. The load-in sucks the big one."

These truck stop interludes also facilitated brief cultural exchanges and the promotion of goodwill among road-weary rock and roll ambassadors.

"I got some good shit here!"

"Right on! Let's check it out!"

Let me take a moment here to explain a little more clearly what a roadie is. A rock and roll roadie qualifies as unique among earth species. To some, the term *roadie* conjures up the image of a guy with big muscles, an I.Q. somewhere between 30 and 60, and a sloped cranium. He is only the second generation in his family to walk erect but he still drags his knuckles on the ground occasionally. He consumes massive quantities of drugs and tries to get at least one blow job from every groupie who shows up at gigs. In fact, to him, doing the shows is only something he has to do in order to pass the time between blow jobs. He constantly complains about being overtired, overworked, underpaid, and homesick, but when a tour ends, the poor wretch goes mental until he's back out on the road. He just can't seem to function in a real-life habitat for want of formal training and a general lack of desire to do so.

Not all of this is true. Some roadies hardly ever get homesick!

Seriously, in later years I've tried to explain to people that many connotations of the term *roadie* are stereotypical and denigrating. All the gentlemen on the ZZ Top crew were *technicians*, not *roadies*. Of course, during my travels I did meet *some* band crewmen who fit the stereotype but soon learned to keep my distance from them. You could never tell whether or not they were diseased, physically or mentally, and you really didn't want to get close enough to find out for sure. They might be contagious.

There was (and still is) a subspecies of roadie called *technical dudes*, who were a breed all their own. A touring band had to have at least one technical dude along in order to *really* repair things that the other roadies only attempted to repair. Technical dudes usually wore the disguise of sound engineer, but I have spotted a few of them posing as lighting engineers and laser operators.

Some technical dudes were the only guys on tour who wouldn't smoke dope or snort coke; and some were the ones who did the most. Nowadays, rock and roll productions have become so intricate and sophisticated that each tour has several technical dudes at their disposal. But in the Stone Age of touring, you were lucky to have one.

Back then it wasn't important how big your show was. All that mattered was the length of your itinerary. Tours never seemed to begin or end: The bands and crews just changed their T-shirt logos. Guys who went to 'Nam came back sooner than some roadies who took off on an overnighter that got extended. Stories about the Grateful Dead's roadies being out there for ten years straight aren't all that much of an exaggeration. Just look at the original Grateful Dead band members that are left, if you require hard evidence.

The managers, agents, and promoters who booked the tours had twisted senses of humor, a bloodlust for money, and absolutely no concept of time or distance. At one of the better-known New York agencies a dollar bill was used to gage distances. If two cities on the wall map were no farther apart than the length of the bill, it was okay to schedule a band to play one after the other on consecutive days, or "back to back." The scale of the map made about as much difference to these armchair geographers as the fact that they were measuring things "as the crow flies" without allowance for the reality that the roadies had to drive up, over, and around minor obstacles such as the Rocky Mountains to get to their destinations.

As far as weather conditions went, shit—everything was always accepted as "perfect" when the scheduling took place. Even if outside the office windows it was July while schedulers were lining up shows for January, the promoters just looked at a current forecast and "booked 'em." When January rolled around, if there *was* a weather problem, these guys acted like it was the fault of the crew that some blizzard had closed down a highway and there was a slim-to-none chance of finishing the last 300 miles of

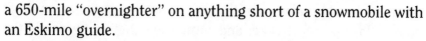

a 650-mile "overnighter" on anything short of a snowmobile with an Eskimo guide.

Somehow ZZ's crew always made it anyway.

During these years, as we ceaselessly crisscrossed the country, Ham would drive the band in rented cars on occasion. Less frequently the Boys would fly. Partly due to his miserly nature, but primarily due to actual limitations of operating capital, flying tended to be a last resort (which was fine with Dusty). The two-or three-man crews did their own driving in rented trucks, since ZZ's gear had long since outgrown my van. Like other bands just starting out, we hadn't reached the money plateau required to hire a semi and driver. We were far from it.

This meant that a road crew on a normal day would work all day setting up the equipment; do a sound check; fix anything that was broken; check what was fixed; have the technical dude fix it again because whoever tried to do it the first time was too tired to think straight; work the performance; tear the gear down after the show; load the truck; then have a big argument over who had to drive first. We did this day after day after day.

The band didn't have it much better. Sometimes Frank and Dusty would ride in the equipment van or PepsiCo truck to get away from Billy and Ham. That was no problem for Billy, because they smoked cigarettes and he didn't. He hated riding in the same car with a smoker, and Frank and Dusty would chain-light one off the next. Back in the truck, Dusty rode along strumming an old guitar and made up music and humorous lyrics for everyone's fun. Frank, Pete, and I would try to join in between fits of laughter. Dusty was always good, but when he was punchy from lack of sleep he was really a riot.

It seemed as though Bill Ham, like all the other promoters and agents, was totally oblivious to the fact that there was no sleep time built into the schedules he cooked up for roadies. Once, out of sympathy, the bandsmen bought us some powdered speed of unknown origin. We were confronting a horrendous power drive from East Jesus Christ to West Godalmighty. I snorted some of this stuff later in front of Billy, right off the top of his wardrobe case. He stared at the performance as if he had just witnessed the assassination of the Maharishi himself. He just knew that it had to be cocaine—a recreational chemical—instead of the intended "business" powder. The band never okayed *that* sort of purchase again on general principles.

Eventually it got to the point where management took it for granted that the crew could take turns sleeping in the truck while en route to the shows. This was totally ridiculous, but as I said in the beginning, Bill Ham wouldn't listen to negativism. The only way a human being (even *homo roadensis noxius*) could sleep in a Ryder "yellow dog" truck was if he was a blind, deaf, dwarf contortionist with no sense of heat, cold, or smell. Those trucks would be a challenge for a Ninja warrior apprentice.

In the summer it was futile to torture yourself with dreams of air-conditioning, because in a Ryder there was none. Plain and simple, summertime meant that you broiled alive. How about rolling down the windows, you ask? We did, of course. But when you rolled down the windows for air, you also allowed into the cab of the truck all the delightful sounds of the great Interstate. There were high-pitched screams from passing trucks, sirens from speeding emergency vehicles, jackhammers from road crews, and screeching brakes from demented motorists. It has been recorded that the noise level inside the cab of a Ryder truck is around 150 decibels, roughly the same as for a jet engine. After we took the governor off the engine to ensure maximum performance, sixty-five miles per hour sounded like Mach I. If you're not hip to decibels, suffice it to say that trying to catch some winks in a Ryder was like trying to take a little snooze cuddled up inside the business end of a Concorde.

Even if the noise problem was circumvented with earplugs, there was the question of space itself. For your total sleeping enjoyment and comfort, you had about three feet of width, three of height, and two of depth in the shotgun slot of your truck. Houdini had more room to work with. During the quest for sleep, more positions would be assumed than those illustrated in the Kama Sutra. If you had the added curse of being tall, as I did, your head generally wound up in the middle of the front seat directly in line with the gearshift knob. If whoever was driving missed a gear, you got whacked directly in the face. And you could forget about straightening your legs.

Since shows finished late and the load-outs were even later, by the time the truck got rolling good the sun was just about ready to rise. It's hard to describe what it's like to be totally exhausted, travelling due east on the ninth morning of twelve in a row, looking directly into a boiling orange fireball through eyes that feel like cracked marbles soaked in alcohol. I wouldn't wish it on Saddam Hussein. Under the best conditions, friendly ol' Mr. Sun beamed down through the windshield directly onto your eyelids, cooking away your retinas with cheerful indifference.

Ah yes, the romance and magnetism of the road.

Let me put in a last word here on roadie lifeways and then move on. I wish to speak of personal hygiene and the en route roadie, and the word is: *odoriferous.*

A roadie didn't have time to shower 'n' shave often. There wasn't much of a chance for social niceties when you were doing nine or ten shows in a row. The cab of the ZZ Top equipment truck developed its own bouquet of delicate fragrances, forming an atmosphere that hasn't supported life forms since the Precambrian. I suppose that gives you some idea of where Pete and I lay in the scheme of Darwinian evolution, so far as management theory went.

After the first couple of days on tour no one ventured near the cab of the truck except the crew. For Pete and me, having gotten used to our noxious environment, this was always something that hurt our feelings a little bit. Stink? What stink? The human olfactory system has an automatic breaker switch, I've learned since then. Amazing odors become tolerable past a certain point of hypersaturation. Lucky thing, because that's the only way we could have survived.

Feet were the main generators of our aroma. Sometimes shoes wouldn't be removed for days at a time, and when they were, MON DIEU! The uninitiated didn't want to be anywhere downwind, much less confined in that cab. Hardworking feet encased for several days in sweaty socks and rubber tennis shoes released an odor similar to mustard gas filtered through rotten tuna. Alas for the unsuspecting hitchhiker, jumping in without knowing what was coming.

"Whew, man! You guys septic tank repairmen? What died? If you don't mind, I'll sit by the window. Jeezus K. Ryst!"

The band once dropped by our room to see us during a rare interlude for R and R in a roadside motel. Friendly grins abruptly downshifted into dismayed grimaces. "Holy shit! What have you morons been rollin' in?"

When they discovered the source of the funk, our shoes were immediately banished to the balcony, and our feet ordered to the showers, but it was no use. The room itself had been permanently tainted after a mere five minutes of roadie occupation. Issuing cries of disgust, Billy, Dusty, and Frank fled for their olfactory lives.

Perhaps there is an industrial or military use for that smell; with proper application it could possibly have shortened the Gulf War, and that's sayin' something.

We weren't unique, of course. These same subhuman conditions existed for all the other crews. We were overtired, aromatic, semicomatose ambassadors of goodwill; expected to work together in perfect harmony on a daily basis. Luckily the vibes from the Age of Aquarius still lingered on, and we pulled it off, for the most part.

Along the way I've mentioned the sums paid to roadies in the beginning stages of ZZ Top's struggle. They weren't much, but Bill Ham and the band weren't making much, either. We all went on the gigs, got our meager pay, then in between most shows roadies held down an array of exotic or mundane jobs to actually pay most of the bills that had been incurred while we "paid our dues." In the music business, you can't really get on your new hoss all at once. You have to stay on the old nag while you wait and hope. In my case, for years I did various things to keep my head above water, keeping the faith that ZZ Top would eventually climb up out of the pack.

Once we reached the stage of power touring, with enough gigs to keep that old cash flow flowing along without any snags, only then did we all quit our jobs and hang with music full-time. We started getting paychecks on a regular basis, a fiscal transformation greeted with considerable satisfaction by the whole team. A grand sense of solid impetus and progress developed, making the weary days and weeks on the road seem more tolerable.

Out in the trenches, it was taken for granted that the roadies would be able to make all the tactical decisions required to pull off a multi-act show without a hitch. Even when a stage just didn't have enough space for everybody's band gear, like that time in Española. This was when management would stand back and let the road crews work out the mundane details by themselves.

After ten or twelve hours of being stir-fried in a Ryder yellow dog navigating bad highways and inclement weather, to arrive somewhere and find a screwed-up stage, electricity problems, or whatever, put everyone's nerves and tempers to a considerable test. Although the shows went on, the logistical follies produced crew wars, or even crew mutinies, more than a few times.

One crew mutiny flared up among the Aerosmith ranks in 1974. ZZ Top had gotten headliner status, with Aerosmith and Dr. Hook and the Medicine Show opening. The problem was that we found ourselves looking at a two-act stage on which we had to set up a three-act show. The promoters had, in typical style, handed us ten pounds of manure to stuff into a five-pound sack. All the roadies were in various stages of exhaustion and ill-temper, none too inclined toward reasoning together the modifications and concessions we needed to implement in order to pull off the evening. Increasingly hot words and descriptive gesturing led to Dr. Hook's roadie Pat "Bubba" Morrow suggesting that it all be worked out in old Viking style: Each crew would choose its biggest guy and space would be granted to whoever was left standing at the end of a round-robin slug-out. This didn't come to pass, largely because of intra-crew arguments over who was "biggest." In ZZ Top's case, we couldn't agree whether Pete, at around three hundred pounds, was bigger than me, at a lanky six foot four. Reason triumphed at last, and with minor flashes of anger and/or frustration, we got the revised sets organized.

Bands were pretty tractable when they arrived and found wildly altered permutations of what they had expected to see set up on stage, but when Steven Tyler of Aerosmith showed up he was *not* a happy camper. He only had a yard of space left in which to caper and prance, and tried to get his crew to enlarge his territory via some pretty arrogant and stupid remarks. At one point he held a glass of liquid over Pete's head, like he would douse him if his will was not adhered to, an act that certainly *would* have started a return to Norse times. He pulled back wisely when he saw Pete's face, and instead gave a toast, raising the drink. "Let the best band win," he said.

Tyler and the rest of Aerosmith did their show without any further altercations. The Aerosmith crew, however, had evidently encountered this sort of thing once too often. At the end of the show they all quit *en masse*—or at least they mutinied for one show and walked off. It was a pleasure that evening to watch the great Steve Tyler, lead singer and star, personally (and almost single-handedly) push gear up the ramp into the Aerosmith truck. Justice was served, at least this once.

Another serious problem developed one night in Denver among the crews of three nations: Golden Earring (Kingdom of the Netherlands), King Crimson (United Kingdom of Great Britain and Ireland), and ZZ Top (Empire of Texas). It started when a Golden Earring roadie shoved me off the six-foot-high stage. The reason was? He thought I had turned on the house lights early to cut their act short so that ZZ could get moving. I went flying off toward some hot power cables, narrowly averting an untimely 600-amp trip to Valhalla. In retribution, Randy Fletcher (whose usual piano key smile had turned into a Velociraptor grimace) grabbed the roadie and attempted to remove his head from his shoulders like a twist-off bottle cap. Dave Rowe got excited and grabbed whoever was closest, who happened to be an innocent King Crimson guy. Skirmishes began erupting all over the stage, with rival roadies pushing and shouting in a confused tangle of hair and machismo. Since the house lights were in fact on, this was all in full view of the audience, which began rooting with enthusiasm. It took several minutes and some large security guards to restore law and order and let ZZ Top play. Some fans said later that the fight alone was worth the price of admission that evening.

This show was also memorable because Billy Gibbons played the whole gig in pain. That afternoon he had cut the middle finger of his left hand while trying to open a can of Mexican hot sauce. The accident required several stitches and did some minor tendon damage, so when time came to perform he was hurting badly and had a splinted, stiff finger to boot. Any other guitarist would have cancelled out, but Billy played anyway, using a slide bar for most of the songs. The promoter, Barry Fey, made an announcement about it prior to ZZ's show, in case Billy had to stop in mid-gig. Therefore, the fans knew what was going on and the applause honoring what he was doing for them was considerable. By taking a risk and making a ballsy appearance Billy gained a lot of respect from everybody.

Yet another roadie skirmish occurred when T-Rex was ZZ Top's opening act. Because Dusty was an asthmatic, and too much smoke made it hard for him to breathe, we asked the head roadie of T-Rex to not use their overdrive flash pot effect. It produced a tremendous amount of acrid smoke and was a pain in the ass anyway. We explained that if Dusty couldn't breathe, he sure couldn't play. Sounds like a reasonable request, doesn't it?

Not to the T-Rex roadie. ZZ Top and Dusty could drop dead: He was going to use the flash pot, and to hell with the consequences. We didn't take kindly to this sort of attitude, no more than any other Southern gentlemen would have. The ZZ Top crew determined that the flash pot would not go off, so Dave Rowe quietly pulled out his Buck knife and made the necessary electrical disconnections after T-Rex started to play.

When the time came to set off the charges, the T-Rex roadie hit his switch and . . . nothing happened. He spun around and spotted our feeble attempts to keep from laughing. Figuring out what was going on, the roadie flat went nuts. That charge was going to go off, and he was going to make sure it happened. As we watched, he traced the wire up to where Dave had snipped it (which was fairly close to the flashpot) and put the two ends together. The only problem with this was that he had neglected to toggle the control switch back to the "off" position.

When he touched those wires together, the pot went off like a Claymore mine. The stage shook, flame and smoke blew sky-high, and the roadie almost had his face peeled off his skull by the detonation. He reeled back with blackened face and singed eyebrows. The ZZ crew had no sympathy for the unhappy roadie at all, and broke up laughing. The guy had gotten what he had coming to him, we all agreed.

But the biker gang that had been hired for "concert security" didn't quite see it that way. For some reason the bikers got it into their heads that we might have intentionally fried the roadie, so they huddled and decided that after the show was over the whole ZZ Top contingent should be prevented from leaving until the truth of the matter could be worked out. For insurance purposes the bikers stationed a bald-headed muscle man at the backdoor. Standing wide-legged with folded arms, he looked like one tough son of a bitch. "It's Kojak on steroids!" I thought.

ZZ Top had its own protection force, though, a former peace officer named Jim Lander. Tonight he was wearing a leather vest and a huge, white Stetson, a veritable rock and roll McCloud. Lander led us toward Kojak at the door, totally unintimidated. As he came up to the biker enforcer he reached his hand underneath the vest, like he was going for his piece. Here was a good example of Texas Tough against Biker Bullyboy. You guessed it: That biker knocked people down running for his life. He even helped clear a path out to the waiting ZZ Top limo.

It was incidents like these that kept Bill Ham always on the lookout for trouble. What happened to John Lennon, getting blasted on a street corner by a weirdo, is always a threat. Notoriety in and of itself brings out psychos and kooks by the score, ready to earn headlines and immortality for having done violence to a rock group or its support troops. One time ZZ Top was invited to fly on Alice Cooper's plane during a tour with him, but Ham declined the offer. He was afraid that somebody fed up with Alice's music and/or style might decide to bomb the plane and take out ZZ Top along with him. Ham tried to keep the Boys and the crew protected as much as possible.

I've been giving you some idea of what life was like as ZZ Top did what had to be done to get a stab at genuine stardom. There was a lot of sweat involved, as I've said; but you have to remember that none of it would have been possible or made any sense if ZZ hadn't been creating some of the best rock and roll music around.

You might say that developing the music and scheduling the gigs were strategic planning back at headquarters in Houston; tactical implementation of these plans was carried out at hundreds of places around the country. Once the process of getting the show together was knocked out, most problems afterward had to do with screwed-up communications and egos.

Here's a good example. Once in Montana it was arranged for

ZZ Top to perform two college shows back-to-back, playing a twin bill with New Riders of the Purple Sage leading off. Now, college shows are generally as likely to produce headaches as anything a radio station puts together for you. It's like there is some unwritten Law of Nature out there which says ALL COLLEGE AND RADIO GIGS WILL BE SCREWED UP. In this particular case the worm in the apple was at the contract level. The college liaison had issued a contract to Bill Ham's company saying that the New Riders would play for no more than forty-five minutes to warm up the audiences. *Then* he proceeded to sign up New Riders, and in their contract it was stated that they would have no less than *seventy-five* minutes to play. That's really too long for an opening act, because the fans can get burned out before the headliners ever hit the stage.

Despite the potential for bruised egos, the first show came off without a hitch between bands or crews. The two crews got along well, and no real time-of-play issue came up because the crowd had been so-so and the New Riders didn't do an encore. They ran a little overtime (by ZZ's contract) but nobody worried about it. That is, nobody worried about it until Pete checked in with Bill Ham back in Houston, pushing paper around in his office. When Pete mentioned the two contract times, and that New Riders had indeed gone past forty-five minutes the first night, Ham turned the phone lines molten. Distilling what he had to say into printable language, it was Ham's very substantial opinion that the New Riders contract didn't mean SHIT and Pete was to make sure the forty-five minute time limit was upheld.

Pete had already found that the female road manager with the New Riders was one of those ladies who was not easily negotiated with by large semi-chauvinist male Texans. Predictably, when Pete dutifully approached her with Ham's dictum she was totally unimpressed. For backup she phoned *her* manager back at the home office. When the situation was outlined for him, his dogmatic opinion was that the *ZZ Top* contract didn't mean shit and that the New Riders should go for their contracted seventy-five minutes.

It all seems pretty childish, doesn't it? Still, long-distance puppeteering like this by men back at headquarters was commonplace, and managerial rigidity caused more flare-ups than they prevented.

Eventually, with college representatives trying to arbitrate things, the New Riders' road manager said that she would agree on a sixty-minute playing time for her band. "No way," Pete said. Having already felt Ham's verbal lash on more than one occasion, he was going to stick absolutely with his orders. So nothing had been settled by the time the auditorium filled and the New Riders kicked off their act.

Montana was right in the middle of New Riders turf, so although their road manager had told them to play short, it came as no surprise when the college kids wanted an encore. The New Riders had already played fifty-five minutes, so to hold within the sixty they *thought* they had, the band remained onstage and got ready to play one last song.

It was at this point that I, down at the lighting controls, heard Pete's voice come on in my headphones, calling down from his perch up in the press box. "Dave, hit the house lights," he said. I tried to reason with him. It was obvious not only that the New Riders deserved an encore but that they were just about to crank up. "Goddamit! Do what I told you!" he said. Grimly I turned back to the panel. It was easy for *him* to give the order. He wasn't down here within a few feet of the fans and the whole New Riders' contingent.

When the lights came up the New Riders guys stopped, blinked, and looked around to see what had happened. The crowd, some 12,000 strong, went from cannabis cool to riot rage in a single instant. The air was filled with booing, screaming, and hurled projectiles. A great roar of disapproval echoed throughout the auditorium. I cringed at what I had done, and more so when the road manager, visibly enraged, appeared beside me and demanded to know what in the hell was going on. I mumbled some lame excuse, trying to sound as dumb as I felt, but she wouldn't buy it. She was so furious she looked like she could have kicked Freddie Krueger's ass.

To add to the situation, now here arrived the head roadie of the New Riders. His face was beet red, the veins in his neck purple and pumped to the diameter of a garden hose. "Where's that FAT mother-FUCK-er?!" he roared. Thank the Lord, the guy didn't want to use my face for a floor polisher; he was after Pete.

Before I could say anything, the roadie turned and bolted for ZZ's dressing room, his face a twisted mask of demonic possession—like Charlie Manson on some bad acid. He threw open the Boys' dressing room door with a hinge-bending bang. Billy, Frank, and Dusty were preparing for their show and turned to stare, clearly having no idea what was going on. No, they sure didn't know where the FAT mother-FUCK-er was. The roadie whirled and fired back toward the stage.

By now the audience had quieted down some. The stage hands were trying to remove the New Riders' equipment without supervision from the two roadies, who were both furiously searching for truth, justice, and Pete's ass.

Then a cry rang out. "THERE'S that FAT mother-FUCK-er!" I turned around just in time to see the New Riders' head roadie dive straight off the stage onto the astonished face of Pete, who had foolishly vacated his safe hiding place and come down to do his preshow routine. The roadie and Pete went down in a tangled mess of flying fists, the roadie doing most of the work upon Pete's head, neck, and shoulders. The brilliant house lights lit up the whole half-time show for the audience, which shouted discordant encouragement to both pugilists.

It took about six stagehands to peel off this *hombre*. Pete staggered back from the straining, cursing roadie, his face drained of color. Unconsciously, his hand reached up to diddle with the acupuncture pin a doctor had recently plugged into his ear to curb his appetite. Every time Pete felt a craving and wanted to eat he was supposed to twist the pin. Judging by the twisting that pin had just gotten, Pete wouldn't be craving anything but pain-killers for two or three weeks.

While the head roadie was getting calmed down, Pete headed safely for the dressing room to check on the band. He was shook up and in bad need of sanctuary. But he only got a couple of steps.

All of a sudden from out of nowhere and straight at Pete's head flew the largest projectile of the evening. Everybody had forgotten about the *other* New Riders' roadie, the *big* one. Now he was stretched out, hurling himself over a table with right arm and fist extended and forming a battering ram. It was a human rocket, a Pete-seeking missile, and dead on target.

The roadie blindsided Pete with a clip on the jaw that would have dropped Mike Tyson, and he collapsed like a circus tent. The crowd roared its approval at the sight of struggling combatants a second time. If they couldn't have more of the New Riders, this was okay as a substitute. The rolling around and punching only lasted a few seconds, however. Even though the new roadie was bigger than his chief, it took fewer people to pull him off. Pete had clearly taken some serious punishment for his crimes, so the point was made. The shouting of the rock and roll audience *cum* heavyweight title rooters died away and in a few minutes ZZ Top started its show.

There were disadvantages to being ZZ Top's production manager, I noticed more than once. Whenever a target of ire was needed by some exasperated or lunatic roadie or fan, Pete stood in the bull's-eye. One night, when Pete was trying to hold down the volume of an opening act, their sound man actually pulled a gun on him. He demanded, and *got*, more volume. Rock and roll can be a serious business indeed.

Pete's funniest payback, at least in the eyes of all the beholders, came in San Francisco at the late Bill Graham's Winterland club. Winterland had its own sound and lighting systems, and any band that played there was expected to use them. This way Mr. Graham was usually able to avoid paying the normal promoter's fee for the sound and lights a band employed on tour. In this case, however, Bill Ham demanded that Graham permit ZZ Top to use its touring equipment, arguing correctly that it was specialized and integral to ZZ's performance. Graham grudgingly gave in after a while and wound up paying his portion of the sound and lighting expenses, but he didn't like it one little bit.

The opener for this show was Commander Cody and the Lost Planet Airmen. ZZ Top's lighting equipment was all set up, the Winterland stuff hoisted up near the ceiling to be out of the way, when up came a Commander Cody roadie lieutenant. He was a burned-out ex-Grateful Dead crewman, and he wanted to use ZZ's backlighting for the Cody show. Pete refused to let him, as is fairly normal. Backlighting is saved for the headliners, so that they can have a little more punch than the openers.

The Cody roadie didn't bat an eye. He began giving instructions to his troops to lower the massive Winterland rig; if ZZ wasn't going to be cooperative, he would just use a substitute. Pete realized that the Winterland equipment dwarfed what ZZ Top had to offer, which would make Cody look a lot more dramatic than Billy, Frank, and Dusty. Rather than be badly out-gunned, Pete compromised with the scraggly roadie. Cody could use the ZZ Top backlighting, but *only one-half of it*. This agreement pacified all concerned, with the minor exception of Cody's production manager, who really still wanted the whole shebang; and Bill Graham, who wasn't around at the time to know what was agreed upon.

Graham in fact didn't become aware of the lighting situation until *during* the Cody show, when he walked over and stood behind Cody's lighting director at the console. I had taken the precaution of taping over the taboo light switches, just to forestall any "accidental" use of them by an errant Cody man, and was also standing by on guard duty.

When Bill Graham saw those taped-over switches he went purely apeshit. No, I take that back. First he calmly asked me what the tape was for. When I told him, *then* he went apeshit.

"I am the OWNah of this place, MissTAHH!" he shouted. "I paid for ALL of these lights, MissTAHHH! Cody WILL use them ALL, MissTAHHHH!"

I felt like the guy in the chair in the Maxell tape ad, with the hot blast of Bill Graham's wrath blowing my hair back. When Graham stopped to take a breath, I started to tell him that my orders came from Pete Tickle, who in turn had gotten his direct from Bill Ham. Before more than a word or two came out, "Misstahh" Graham informed me that if I spoke one more syllable I could stick my lighting console up my ass and walk out the back door with it.

Now there's imagery to give pause. Graham had a real knack for turning a phrase.

After my hair stopped streaming out and my face had begun to cool, common sense bid me heed the man's request. No, it was fear of a lighting console enema that made discretion win over valor. Fuck valor! Valor can get your ass kicked.

Now began a neo-"Saturday Night Live" scenario. I found Ham back in the dressing room and told him what was up. Ham jumped up from his chair in a fury. He said when I saw Graham again to say that Bill Ham was looking for him, then sat back down to whatever he was doing. So I shuffled back to the stage. At the set change I spotted Bill Graham and went over to pass on Ham's message. Before I could get a word out, Graham told me in a tight voice to tell Bill Ham that *he* was looking for *him*!

Well, Ham and Graham "looked" for each other all night but never hooked up. If you've ever been to Winterland you might find this to be a little strange, because it's not that vast a complex. It wasn't as if they were on different sides of Disney World or anything. No, it was just two old rock and roll dogs circling each other at a safe range, vicariously sniffing each other's assholes. If you never come together, you don't get bit — real simple.

Meanwhile, ZZ Top stormed the stage and ended all questions of who was and who wasn't the headliner. The show went on in grand form, without a glitch until close to the end. During one of the last songs, one of the headset "call" buttons on the lighting console started blinking like a strobe light. I saw that it was Pete's headset, based at the soundboard. When *that* one went off, it usually spelled bad trouble with the sound. Randy Fletcher rushed over to answer the call on our headset, listened intently for a second, then threw the headset down and broke up in fits of convulsive laughter. He eventually composed himself and explained to me what the light meant.

It seemed that the old Cody roadie, still irritated about the whole lighting exchange, had carried out a raid. While Pete was intently mixing the sound, the guy sneaked up behind him, reached around, and smushed a full plate of red beans and rice into Pete's face before hauling ass. It made one hell of a mess, all over Pete and all over the soundboard. Pete was combing beans and rice out of his eyes and nose, spluttering for Randy to drop everything and go kick the roadie's ass. No luck there; even if he had wanted to, Randy had to do a guitar change with Billy in about a minute. Jerry Cameron, our sound engineer and technical dude at the time, had been standing next to Pete and witnessed the whole thing. He laughed so hard he nearly passed a kidney stone.

The perpetrator of the red beans caper was never brought to justice. Ham and Randy stormed into the Cody dressing room after the show to search it while the band members and their numerous guests silently looked on, but the roadie had made tracks. Pete had to put up with the knowledge that this was the one guy who'd gotten away.

So much for sampling what it was like to be perpetually on the road during the 1970s. There was so much touring it got to the point where the music was almost an afterthought to the adventures as we sat around and reminisced. It was plates of beans in our faces that we remembered, not where it was that Billy tried an extra riff in "Thunderbird" or Dusty sang minor harmony in something else. Like with all professional work, the work itself gets to be so familiar that it becomes just another part of living; kind of like bad breath.

There was no time for complacency, though. Bill Ham was cooking up another major step forward for ZZ Top as the 1970s reached their midpoint.

PART III

RUNNIN' HARD

8

THE BARNDANCE AND BARBEQUE

The creation of a rock and roll tour is analogous to pregnancy and birth. It all starts with the tiny seed of a tour concept, which then impregnates the mother-to-be's waiting egg. After conception, the tour idea begins to grow, passing through a gestation period of several months. During this time the anxious parents—the band and manager—go temporarily insane wondering what to name it, what it will look like, and how successful it will be in life.

In ZZ Top's case, the *paternity* of tours was attributable to a musical seed planted by the band. *Maternity* was Bill Ham's department. He was the "hungry mutha" who in turn carried the developing tour idea in his brain, presented to the world, and then nurtured it carefully after birth and during growth.

When the joyous day arrives for a rock and roll tour to be born, the infant bursts free from the womb of warehouse and rehearsal hall for all the world to see and judge. But as with human infancy, this is only the beginning. Proud parents must begin the laborious task of educating and improving the child, including teaching it how to walk and talk. The parents hope and pray that all who come and see their offspring will love it like they do, and say how cute it is.

And as with a human child, a rock and roll tour must eventually be taught not to shit in its own pants. That's the tough part.

Bearing all of this in mind, the origins of the ZZ Top World Wide Texas Tour in 1976 closely paralleled the birth and development of the Elephant Man. There was a long pregnancy, a hard labor, and a breech delivery. Plus the poor thing was illegitimate because nobody would admit to being the father. The infant was a slow learner, and there were times when it should have been given up for adoption. Even after it reached maturity it still occasionally dropped a load in its trousers.

ZZ Top's World-Wide Texas Tour was conceived because of the inordinate success of a production Ham envisioned in 1974. ZZ had begun to move into the "upper middle class" of rock by this time. The combination of power touring and strategic release of albums almost every year after 1970—not to mention the wildly exciting style of the band's music—had begun to generate some healthy cash flow for ZZ Top and its minions, for which everybody was plenty thankful. It was around this time that Ham got to talking about creating a major outdoor show somewhere. A lot of one-day "celebration of life" productions were being thrown together, yielding a great deal of money. Most notorious of these in Texas was Willie Nelson's Fourth of July Picnic, a semi-country western, semi-progressive country, semi-rock and roll musical whirlwind with a knock-down, drag-out beer bust and mandatory dope smoke. Heck, why shouldn't ZZ Top host a great rock-a-thon? And so ZZ Top's First Annual Texas Size Rompin' Stompin' Barndance and Barbeque came to pass.

I don't think any of the band or crew had a clue as to what to expect when it all started off (appropriately enough) on Labor Day 1974. The Barndance was scheduled to be held in Austin, Texas, two days after a gig we did in Atlanta. That whole extra day made the crew kind of crazy; we *had* to pay a visit to the Electric Factory, then the hottest rock and roll club in Atlanta, where Gregg Allman was playing that night. Since there was a whole day off between shows, and only about a thousand miles between Atlanta and Austin, shit—there was time to burn!

One problem came up when it was time to depart, because somebody in Gregg Allman's entourage decided to play hide-and-seek with Billy Gibbons' gold Halliburton briefcase. Billy had forgotten to load it into his wardrobe case for transit to Austin, so he handed the thing to the crew to avoid messing with it on the plane. Some suspicious people might imagine that since he was a rock and roll guitar player, there were drugs in that briefcase. Rest assured, there weren't any. (I had hoped there were, so I checked.)

Alex Cooley, owner of the Electric Factory and also a promoter with whom we had become friends, stashed the briefcase for us in his office while the crew went and said hidee to the denizons of the local rock animal kingdom. No way were we going to leave that thing in the truck to get stolen! Confident that all would be well, we went and enjoyed ourselves to the max.

But when we came back at closing time, the briefcase had vanished! Remorse, guilt, and paranoia struck deep. Here Billy had trusted us with his briefcase and we had gone and blown it. It was a case of universal misery as the crew rummaged around in hopes that the briefcase would suddenly pop up into plain view.

Presently cooler and in some cases alcoholically wizened heads began to develop a theory about the missing briefcase. Let's see, *we* had been in the office; *Alex* had been in the office; *who else* had been there? Since the Gregg Allman Band had played the

119

club that night, it didn't take a flying team from the FBI to figure where to start our investigations.

We went next door to the hotel where the Allman people were staying the night and talked to a few guys we knew from back in the Allman Brothers Band days. By then we were absolutely certain we knew what had happened, so we told them that all we wanted was the briefcase, no questions asked. I have to admit that while we were talking we all had kind of uninvitedly walked into the room and were conducting an un-search-warranted search, which produced some tension. Then, miraculously, the briefcase appeared. Evidently it had been picked up by mistake by someone who *thought* he had a Halliburton custom-made just like it.

Yeah. Well, mistakes do happen. We shook hands and headed out.

The ZZ Top truck pulled out of Atlanta at around 4:00 A.M., driven by bone-weary, semi-drunk, but totally satisfied-to-be-off-the-hook roadies pleased to have finally located Billy's briefcase. The twenty-hour-plus drive to Austin was uneventful. And always, the never-ending stream of highway stripes attacked us from the horizon with measured precision and no sign of ever letting up. Watching those stripes on a long trip can have a very hypnotic affect. Perspectives become distorted in road-weary minds; you get to the point where you feel as if you were standing still and the planet is rotating under you, instead of you crawling across its surface. Of course, ingestion of miscellaneous mind-expanding chemicals helps to effect this illusion.

ZZ had gotten into Austin the day before; the crew and equipment arrived about 1:00 A.M. on the morning of the Big Gig. This was to be a stadium soiree, meaning a whole lot more people than under usual circumstances. Ham had also put together a strong lineup of supporting acts—Santana, Joe Cocker, and Bad Company. He hoped this would help the Labor Day turnout.

The closer we got to Memorial Stadium on the University of Texas campus, the more people we saw walking the streets and milling around. We were puzzled over what was keeping so many people out on the streets at that hour, but college towns are pretty strange places ordinarily, so we just wrote it off as a typical holiday crowd doin' the rounds. Now we started passing a startling array of tents, pitched all over the place right in the middle of town on yards, in small parks—anywhere. What was this? A hippie jamboree? Was the Greatful Dead doing a show, too? We couldn't tell.

Then the lights of the stadium were directly ahead, and the sight slapped some intelligence into the occupants of the ZZ equipment truck. Hey, *we* were the attraction! ZZ Top and the other bands, that is. These people were hanging around to see the crew performance, too! At least, since we had the responsibility of making everything go, that's the way we felt about it.

The amount of activity going on inside the stadium in the wee hours was more than surprising. Lights and sound were being assembled and hoisted into place, parts of the stage were still being constructed, risers were being painted, and generally there was controlled chaos everywhere you looked. The main eye-catcher was the enormous expanse of playing field, now being covered in its entirety with separate layers of plastic and tarpaulin. That included the end zones and surrounding track, making for one pretty astounding amount of square footage.

The reason for all this attention was that the football field's brand new Astroturf had just been installed; so recently that the University of Texas Longhorns hadn't even practiced on it. You have to realize that this was *Texas*, and Memorial Stadium was hallowed ground. In the past, nothing but Longhorn football games had ever taken place here except for one or two anti-'Nam rallies years before. What Bill Ham and ZZ Top were pulling off at Memorial Stadium was tantamount to holding a sock hop at Arlington National Cemetery, with the bandstand set up on top of the Tomb of the Unknown Soldier. Many old 'Horns regarded this to be the grossest form of sacrilege.

It was later revealed to me that all this came to pass by total accident. Barry Leff, the U. of T. Student Activities Committee President, managed to get the proposal for the show past the

Alumni Committee, the Faculty Committee, the Athletic Committee, and so on upward through the various other committees without a negative remark. No one said no, probably thinking that somebody else would do the dirty work and take the flack for it. Because of this passing of the buck, much to the chagrin and surprise of the various committeemen, the gig was on, even though none of them particularly wanted it.

When he got the news of what was coming, Darrell Royal, the U. of T. Head Football Coach and Athletic Director at the time, was upset to say the least. Here he had just gotten brand-new Astroturf for his gargantuan lambs to exercise on, and now he was going to have to sit back and watch it be subjected to the whims, follies, and bodily functions of tens of thousands of dope-crazed hippies. It was loathsome to the tenth power! Royal was always a "take charge" type—that's one of the things that made him the powerhouse coach he was for years—and it seems he resolved to do his best to torpedo the whole affair. There was language in the proposal which said in so many words that the playing field had to be "properly protected" from damage, otherwise no mass audience would be permitted into Memorial Stadium. Royal would try to make it as tough as possible for the promoters to live up to this part of the agreement. Maybe he should have thrown in a morality clause.

The all-star promoter lineup, a first and only one-shot deal, consisted of Bill Graham (San Francisco), Barry Fey (Denver), Terry Bassett (Dallas), Alex Cooley (Atlanta), and Don Fox (New Orleans). Bill Ham liked to refer to these men as the Big Five. The first four were already well-known in the entertainment industry, but Don Fox was a relative newcomer. His production company was just beginning to establish itself as a major force in the South, and he was also the youngest of the group. Bill Ham liked Don Fox's brash methods and energy; the two of them thrived on bucking the establishment. Probably for this reason, and to shock the other four promoters, Ham put Fox in charge of the Memorial performance. This was actually okay with the others; if there was a disaster, the fingers would be pointed at Fox, not them.

This was how it came to be that Don Fox and crew were the ones who had to deal with ol' Darrell as he made his gambit to bust the whole gig. Darrell perched himself high up in the press box of the stadium, a vantage point from which he kept a bird's-eye view of everything that was going on down there on his Astro-turf. As I said, it seemed to us that if he could torpedo the whole event, that would be fine with him.

Coach Royal had already managed to hold up Fox's activities twice for inconsequential reasons. Now, on the evening before Labor Day, Royal played his hand: a Royal flush, so to speak. "In his professional opinion" as athletic director, the only way the playing field could be adequately protected was to have the whole thing covered, in addition to the plastic and tarps, with *three-quarter-inch plywood*! Talk about your basic insurmountable demand with which to hit the production staff at midnight. The audience, already *camped* outside by the tens of thousands, was supposed to cheer the bands in half a day's time. The gates would be opening at noon on Labor Day. That gave Ray Compton, Don Fox's production manager, only twelve short hours to find, buy, and lay out hundreds of sheets of acceptable plywood and parry Coach Royal's challenge. It was about as impossible a task as could have been thrown at Compton, and I'm sure Darrell Royal went to bed with a smile, content that his Royal flush would beat any cards played by the opposition. Don Fox's production team appeared to be about a dime short on a nickel bet.

If Ray Compton *couldn't* come up with a solution, there would be four internationally known bands, four managers, five promoters, and seventy or eighty thousand fans ready to lynch him as high as the Memorial Stadium scoreboard. There would be a massive catastrophe on the financial front, too. Over a million dollars in ticket sales would go down the toilet, and there would be massive expenses left to pay. Even if he lived to tell the tale, Ray's future in the music business would be blacker than

123

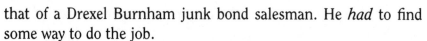

that of a Drexel Burnham junk bond salesman. He *had* to find some way to do the job.

What Ray Compton did to foil the Machiavellian Royal was a stroke of pure, desperate genius. His hand held a wild card— namely his attitude and strong instincts for self-preservation. He jumped into his pickup truck, tore down to the nearest lumber yard, and drove into and over the security gate, thereby setting off the burglar alarm. Within a few minutes squad cars piled into the yard to find Compton calmly leaning against his pickup as he waited for them. The cops approached him cautiously—what was this freak up to, anyway? In a few words he outlined his problem and asked for them to call the lumber yard owner, which had already been done as a matter of course. This individual arrived shortly thereafter, and came over to see what in the hell was going on down there. Compton pulled out a wad of bills and ticked off about $15,000 in cash. Would the yard owner sell him the plywood Compton needed, and let him pay for the gate?

"Why, hell yes, boy! Why didn't you just phone me yourself?" Sold!

Back at the stadium, around 9:00 A.M., plywood was being put into place by the physically largest and probably most expensive collection of common laborers ever seen together in one place at one time. After Ray Compton left the lumber yard man furiously telephoning his truck force, he went straight back to the stadium to get his army of workers organized to lay the sheets of plywood when they arrived. Luckily he had already lined up players from the University of Texas Football Team for heavy work. Good music had overcome faithfulness to football; much of the team pulled on their sweats, laced up their shoes, and jogged over to the stadium to lend a hand. And when the plywood showed up, the behemoths worked like Trojans to beat the deadline. As part of their reward, Compton benevolently let the football heroes walk on the Astroturf once before it was covered, so they could see what it was like before the new carpet got totally trashed.

When Darrell Royal learned that his own troops had mutinied and were helping the roadies, he folded his cards. Compton had beaten Royal's flush, and only a few of the encamped horde ever knew how perilously close to a cancellation matters had come.

The day of music that followed was a one-day Woodstock, Texas-style. The better part of a hundred thousand music fans made the scene, a bigger turnout than some of the football games played in Memorial. The downside was that this many people—double the estimate—really hadn't been expected even in the wildest dreams of the promoters. This meant that there wasn't enough of anything for the fans. From the promised free barbeque to toilet seats, there was a shortage of everything.

The lack of food and ice and drinks was solved democratically by the crowd in the early phases of the afternoon. After irritation reached a certain point, the vending stands were overrun and whatever remained in tanks and freezers was handed out free of charge. But to make a clear demonstration of disapproval at the poor planning necessitating this step, the crowd also proceeded to tear out a major percentage of the lavatory fixtures and hurl them aside. This was poor planning on the *crowd's* part!

As the masses of concertgoers poured into Memorial, making it clear that this was to be a day to remember, Bill Ham walked by the stage grinning from ear to ear and moving fast. I looked up from some task, wondering where he was going just as the gig of gigs was breaking out.

He said, quite earnestly, "I'm on m' way to the Guv'nor, boy! Gonna try and git him t' bring on the Boys!"

Bill Ham, promoter and manager *extraordinaire*, actually thought he might be able to wangle the Honorable (and most conservative) Dolph Briscoe, Governor of the State of Texas, into stepping out onstage before 80,000 or more rock and roll lunatics to introduce ZZ Top—ZZ Top, most of whose music advocated hard drinkin', hard druggin', and free lovin'. And to a frantic throng of youngsters, the majority of whom had and were ingesting and injecting illegal substances into various parts of their bodies. You have to admit: Bill Ham was a man with a vision.

Jay Boy Adams opened the show with a brief acoustical set. Bad Company followed, with Jimmy Page from Led Zeppelin trying to jam on the encore while tripping on acid. Then came Joe Cocker, able to make it through his set all the way without passing out. The roar of the crowd could be heard all over Austin as the fans shouted and danced like something out of pagan Rome.

Then Santana came on at sundown. It was an eerie moment. The sun was low on the horizon and cast an orange glow over the tortured faces of the sun-drained, drugged-out, straining crowd. The mass of young humanity gathered in the stadium generated dingy gray ripples of body heat that slithered upward like earthbound snakes of energy writhing toward the heavens. Carlos Santana, dressed in pristine white, walked purposefully to the center of the stage, extended his arms with palms together like a child in prayer, and moved his hands slowly back and forth, systematically blessing the crowd. He had all the grace and impact of the Pope at Vatican City on High Holy Day. If you weren't doing any chemicals, it was still a mind-blower. The poor suckers who *were* tripping in the front ranks are probably still preaching somewhere. Santana primed the audience for the main event with his presence and his usual musical intensity. You could feel the coils winding tight throughout the whole scene.

At last, hours after it all had started, it was ZZ Top's turn. Because it was a special occasion, the stage was decorated with hay bales, an old wagon wheel, a cow skull, and some live (if sunstroked) chickens. By God, this sumbitch was a PRODUCTION! It was the first glimmering of what THE WORLD-WIDE TEXAS TOUR was to become, even if Ham had failed to get Governor Briscoe to come down and help out.

From the vantage point of the stage you could take it all in. The entire crowd was on its feet in anticipation. A large portion was chanting "Z . . . Z . . . TOP! Z . . . Z . . . TOP!" The air was charged with heavy emotional electricity, but for the moment it was comparatively subdued and under control. ZZ was following strong competition, but it was obvious who the audience had come to see.

When the stadium lights went down, thousands of cameras focused to freeze an image of the band, and a moment in time. Flashbulbs began exploding, expending tiny flickers of white-hot energy, like stars winking at you from a stadium-sized universe. There was a deafening roar from the crowd, exhausted but rallying. It continued until the Boys hit their first note.

ZZ Top launched into "Thunderbird" like a nitro-burning funny car. The first lyrics were, "Get high, everybody, get high!" But the listeners by and large needed no urging. They were already dizzy with drugs, music, dehydration, and excitement. Adding to the total effect was the way Billy was dressed. He wore a suit from Nudie's Western Tailors, the kind with more sequins on it than you see on amateur night at the Grand Ole Opry. It was the first time for this flashy rig, and it marked a new phase in ZZ stage costuming; for the next couple of years they would be at the height of "chic"; urban cowboys on a lightning bolt.

Their whole show and multitude of encores in Memorial Stadium maintained an intensity unmatched to that point in the Boys' careers. ZZ Top completely used up what was left of the audience's capacity to inundate itself in the rock and roll experience. After an hour and a half set, and a rumbling, roiling double encore, the Boys left the stage and the day was over.

Now people were filing out, some stumbling or even being led. Some were crawling out. Some were just plain out—cold, that is. It took forever before all that was left were the roadies and a few derelict figures here and there. We just sat on the stage and watched them go, like we were reality and *they* were an act.

After a while we came out of our stupors and peered across the University of Texas' field of football gore and glory. In the bright lights of the stadium we could see clearly what ZZ Top and the other bands, through their fans, had wrought. Darrell Royal, if he was up in his press box staring down too, must have looked like a post-trauma shock victim.

The place was totally fucked up.

The playing field looked like a Gulf War battle zone. Besides the mountains of garbage, there were smoldering ashes where fires had been laid, and little plumes of smoke were leisurely curling their way upwards into the night sky. Large pieces had been hacked out of the brand new Astroturf. The next morning, the Austin *American-Statesman* featured a photograph of the playing field which showed a section carved (or burned) out in the shape of Texas. Poor old Darrell's worst fears had come to pass.

Thus ended the initial spark that eventually would lead to the creation of the World-Wide Texas Tour. Hysterical, frantic, heart-palpitating rock and roll at its most dramatic had been played. A mountain of cash higher than anything Bill Ham had ever hoped for had come out of it for ZZ Top. Had any of us taking down the stage and carrying away the gear been there as he drove slowly away from the ruins of what had been the Longhorns' football field, we might have seen him stroking his beard in thought.

Show bidness! Now wasn't that somethin'? Mercy Miss Percy!

I'll wager we could do it again. But why do it just *once*? Why not line up a whole slew of these things, end to end? It'd be like nothing the world ever saw before. Why, we'd have more money comin' in than a television evangelist . . .

So must have gone the thoughts, and so WWTT was conceived. So let it be written; so let it be done.

9

THE ZZ TOP WORLD-WIDE TEXAS TOUR

It didn't take long for Bill Ham to get things moving toward the creation of a rootin' tootin' successor to the Barndance and Barbeque Show. In 1975 he organized the Thank You, Texas Tour, which really wasn't as big as he would have preferred, but it was big enough. The tour would hit five of the biggest cities in Texas—Houston, Dallas, Fort Worth, San Antonio, and Lubbock. The theme read simply enough: ZZ Top was offering a special thanks to all the loyal fans in Texas who had supported it so well, so long. There was no doubt that ZZ *did* owe a lot, and that the Boys felt special about doing a Texas tour. There's also no doubt that a part of the tour's reason for existence was the need for some quick cash to support the *next* tour, which would *really* be an extravaganza.

For Thank You, Texas, Ham and the Boys wanted to create a down-home atmosphere onstage. This was going to be accomplished by scattering a few genuine Texas artifacts (i.e., old saddle, cow skull, wagon wheel, some cedar fencing) and some Texas flora (cactus, yucca, fake boulders) on top of a "typical" Texas land-scape—white linoleum painted to look like a section of desert crossed by the Rio Grande. This last was custom-painted by Bill Narum, who had done some album covers for ZZ Top and was therefore a natural choice for the job. Nobody suggested anything about a landscape of Gulf Coastal buffalo grass, or one of the Big Thicket, or any of the other "typical" landscapes of a greatly var-ied state. Texans themselves buy the stereotypes of Texas even when they know they don't mean squat.

Well, the artifacts looked like artifacts, and the flora looked like flora, and the ZZ Top music was great no matter what, but the linoleum desert just didn't make it. Instead of looking like the mighty Rio Grande meandering through the badlands, the lino-leum gave the impression that someone had spilled a bucket of perfectly good blue paint on a dropcloth, evidently borrowed from some color-blind apartment complex painting crew specializing in hues of brown and beige. Bill Narum's ZZ Top album covers had been pretty good, but *this* was about as close to quality as a reproduction of the *Mona Lisa* on the side of a New York subway car.

The landscape was so pathetic that by the evening of the next-to-last show in Dallas, Pete Tickle felt like venturing a public statement on the matter. Obliquely, retaining sentiment while abandoning clarity, he scribbled on the canvas in black marker, "Narum is Gay." This was a great witticism in Pete's mind, al-though total bullshit; Narum was along on the tour and had his wife with him. For some infantile reason the rest of the crew found humor in the scrawled graffiti anyway. Pete handed the marker to Randy Fletcher, whose Etonian mind yielded the time-lessly poetic legend of "upchucked piña colada." The general hi-larity *that* produced in the assembled roadie population made it inevitable that the rest of us would get into the act. Dave Rowe rivaled Confucian wisdom with his "Five-day-old pizza makes me puke," and I with Sartresque delicacy of implication finished our composition with "This floor ain't fit to wipe a sick moose's hole with." All was inane, but all was harmless; it was the sort of merry pranksterism that produced adornment of cave walls in south France 40,000 years ago, and toilet doors yesterday in a truck stop men's room.

Our superiors did not agree.

Immediately after the Dallas show, Narum's wife hauled Bill Ham onstage and pointed out the insults. Some task of set demolition had carried me to the vicinity, and I was the first to see what was developing. There was no time to become invisible; Ham came up and asked with intensity who had written on the linoleum. Why can't I ever think up a quick, believable lie when the heat is on me? Instead of deflecting the looming danger, I said that it was "some of the crew members." The feces hit the fan blades on the spot. In a tight voice Ham said that anybody who had written something was fired as of right now, then he stalked off the stage, heading for ZZ's dressing room, leaving us with our mouths open.

It was hard to believe that Ham really meant to give walking papers to the only guys on the planet who could set up and run the show. You see, each and every set is a masterpiece of parts wired, duct-taped, and bubble-gummed together. Learning how it all works is like memorizing the wiring schematic of the space shuttle. Nobody but the experienced, trained crew could haul everything to the last show, put it all together again, and then make it all go away. The crew was confused, uncertain. Exactly what kind of "fired" were we? Do we go to the next show and quietly go about our business, then slink away, never to be heard from again? Or should we leave the gear sitting in Dallas and let Bill Ham figure out the next step? And what were we being fired for, anyway, huh? Sabotage? Creating a public nuisance? Abusing fine art? Hell, no. We were just guilty of writing silly graffiti. It was like a death sentence for throwing a spitball. The punishment did *not* fit the crime.

Billy, Frank, and Dusty were pretty concerned, too. They were the ones who would be up to their asses in electrical alligators tomorrow night if the set: (a) wasn't working right; (b) didn't have personnel who knew the show; or (c) hadn't budged from Dallas! What to do, what to do. This predicament had us scratching our heads like a shade tree mechanic staring at a Jaguar engine. Finally, the four ZZ Top roadies, not certain whether this was their last hurrah coming up, pulled the set apart, packed it up in the truck, and pointed northwest for Lubbock. What the hell, we were pros, so let's finish the tour and *then* start thumbing through the rock and roll classifieds.

We arrived in Lubbock for stage call the next morning to find another band's crew waiting to take our places. Point Blank had been added to Bill Ham's stable of bands in Houston awhile before, and in the middle of the night he phoned telling the Point Blank roadies to get their butts to Lubbock for the ZZ Top finale. That's a pretty healthy drive, incidentally; remember, we're talking *Texas*. Lubbock is Hell and gone up on the Staked Plains. The Point Blank roadies had driven all night at top speed from Dallas, and they had made it. Of course, now they were wasted zombies for their efforts, and had no more idea of what to do next than Ronnie Reagan at a press conference without his cue cards.

Well, what the hell, again. We told the exhausted Point Blank crew to stay out of the way. Then our exhausted crew put it all together one more time.

We handled the setup as promised, and went ahead to handle the show itself, too. It all went okay, if with a surreal sensation about it, almost as if the show was going on but we weren't really there playing our technical parts. Billy, Frank, and Dusty did their thing, but in subdued fashion (if a raging rockorama can ever be described that way). They were wondering whether Ham really meant it and if this was the last they would see of us. That included Pete, the top dog roadie, Billy's friend but the criminal agitator who had started the whole affair.

I don't recall seeing Ham all day or at the performance, but

132

after the show was finished he materialized out of nowhere and said he wanted to have a little talk with us. The lecture was brief and to the point. Ham said he had wanted to teach us a lesson—don't trifle with an artist's feelings—and he hoped we had learned it. He smiled a benevolent smile that would have made Jack Nicholson envious. To the Boys' great relief, the perplexity of the Point Blank roadies, and our amazed indignation, Ham informed us that we were rehired. We could go ahead and start pulling the set apart and get on back to Houston. Then he was gone, as magically as he had arrived.

Don't trifle with an artist's feelings? What about *our* feelings? Well, what the hell, a third time. See how it works? Who says it's hard to get into the music business? We'd been in it, out of it, and back in it in less than twenty-four hours.

"Cowboy chic" became a fad in the mid-1970s. Drugstore cowboys were all over the place. Western stores opened up and down the East Coast, filled with imitations of the clothing and paraphernalia believed by anyone who had gone to the movies to see what real bronc busters and wranglers used back when the West was won—designer jeans; tailored, sequined shirts; and ostrich boots. Realizing that things were peaking in the ersatz boots 'n' saddles department, and making the connection between ZZ Top being a Texas band and the Western lunacy, Ham and the Boys began to stitch together ideas for a much-improved, kick-ass tour a lot bigger and badder than the Thank You, Texas quicky. While shitkicker culture was a hot item, this temporary national insanity could provide the basis for a unique tour indeed.

The character and qualities of the impending extravaganza began to germinate as meetings were held between Ham, the Boys, the crew, and representatives of various production companies. There was a cushion of money now because of the Thank You, Texas performances, and more could be located if necessary.

We all began to get excited, anxious, and off-the-wall creative. Some ideas we dreamed up turned out to be better than others. The name of the tour, for example, was pretty good: The ZZ Top World-Wide Texas Tour. But after that there were some real questionable selections.

The first seemingly cockeyed notion that Ham locked in was to incorporate a full-sized steer into the production. Actually, I could see it. There's nothing like a steer to make people think of Texas. Trouble was, a steer is one hell of a big animal. Where could we put it? Not out in front—can't see the band that way, plus the Boys might wind up stepping in something. But if it's to one side of the stage, that throws off the whole symmetry of the set. "What about puttin' a buffalo on the other side?" someone proposed. This raised an eyebrow or two: the Lone Star State represented by a *buffalo*? As we watched, Ham turned the idea over in his head. Before we knew it, a buffalo was on the list of production items. "Better than a herd of armadillos," I thought to myself. The steer came with the name of Texas; for balance in all things, the buffalo was named Tex. Whew! Bet some poor bastard was up all night laboring through that creative process.

This was just the start of things. With a steer and a buffalo already established as part of the show, adding other gimmicks in the same vein was natural. Over the next few weeks, the tour "concept" began to grow and flourish with animalia. In addition to the bovine contingent, ZZ wound up with two large rattlesnakes, a couple of good-sized tarantulas, some buzzards, and an irregular guest appearance by a tightrope-walking baby javelena named Chapo. Barnum & Bailey didn't have a thing on Bill Ham for instincts.

Actually there was some solid thinking behind having all the critters around. They guaranteed massive amounts of free press coverage wherever ZZ Top rambled. Ham and the Boys had been keeping track of acts that had taken to touring with the idea of animals onstage and all this amounted to was Texas-sized elaboration on a theme. Alice Cooper had his boa constrictor, Ozzy Osborne had his bats—but ZZ Top was bringing home the beef!

The big steer and buffalo were originally stationed on fixed platforms constructed to either side of the stage. That sounds simple, but it wasn't. Those platforms were about as easy to assemble as an oil derrick. It took more time and stagehands to put them together than the Great Pyramid of Cheops, so after the first few shows they were abandoned in favor of movable, motorized lifts. Either way, the cost of the whole shebang was astounding. For a total presentation time of around ninety seconds per show, before the steer and buffalo were whisked into safe seclusion, the tour shelled out several hundred thousand dollars. It was figured that the frantic press they generated still made them well worth it all.

The other animals were less of a trial. The buzzards rotated appearances and when in action were tethered on a perch behind Dusty's speakers. The snakes got a position at center stage in a padlocked Plexiglas dome as close to the front row as possible. Needless to say, there weren't any security problems in this area! The tarantulas started off the tour on display in the ZZ Top hospitality room. I say "started" because they didn't finish the tour. The poor critters turned out not to be too roadworthy and expired early on.

The stage set, designed by Brian Marshall, was a real masterpiece of invention. It was to be shaped roughly like the state of Texas, sloped toward the audience at four degrees so that this could better be made out during concerts. It was to be thirty-two feet wide, twenty-four feet deep, and able to fit on top of any pre-existing stage. After being set up, we would scatter here and there over the whole thing surviving props from the Thank You, Texas Tour—the cow skull, the wagon wheel, the yucca plants—and some new, handier fake boulders. The finishing touch to all this would be a thirty-six-foot-wide by twenty-foot-tall three-dimensional backdrop panorama of an arid landscape, consisting of four layers of netting contrived to look like a deep west-Texas valley,

135

complete with mountain. Special lighting effects would make it burn with the fever of a west Texas sunset or shiver under the icy gaze of a midnight moon, surrounded by stars scattered through the heavens like diamond buckshot. Shee-it! Nothing like this had ever been pulled off before, and the thought of it all blew our minds.

Let's see: longhorn steer, buffalo, rattlesnakes, buzzards, tarantulas, Texas-shaped stage, 3D panorama. . . . That ought to do it. This stuff looked *real* good on paper. Now all we had to do was build it. It took months of phone calls, consultations with contractors, revisions, headaches . . . and lots and lots of money. As all the parts began to be assembled, the band and crew started to have more of a feel about what it would be like when completed. There was also an inevitable squirreliness in our stomachs, too. Here was all this stuff piling up in the warehouse. Sooner or later it would have to be used.

LIGHTS! CAMERA! MUSIC! By God, it was time for a dress rehearsal!

Bill Ham had scouted around Houston for a good place to do this, and finally hit on the idea of renting the Astro Arena next to the Astrodome. It was the only place in town big enough. So with great fanfare, on the first morning of ZZ's allotted week, up to the Arena we all came with truckloads of parts, tools, people, and animals. The rock and roll circus had come to town for sure, complete with sideshow of freaks and carnies with bull horns. Ham had grumbled about having to take the arena for a full week; he mistakenly imagined that all we had to do was nail a few boards and tighten down a few nuts. As it happened, the week was barely long enough to get the ZZ Top act together.

We immediately discovered that none—NONE—of the parts of the show fit together right, and we would have to build that sucker practically from scratch right then and there. Everything was wrong. The inside of the Astro Arena dissolved into a swirling, churning maelstrom of work crews, parts of sets, musicians, tools, and whatnot. It was a melting pot of emotions and high stress. At any given instant you could hear frantic shouting, hysterical accusations, paranoid bursts of cussing, and blasts of rehearsal music. Nothing worked, nothing fit, and there was chaos in every cranny. The nooks were taken up by animals.

We first managed to succeed in hoisting up that immense panoramic backdrop—and found that with optimum lighting, pressed to the max and beyond, it looked like the world as it must appear to a purblind myope—reality through a dirty window. In other words, it was a piece of shit. Unfortunately, it was paid for, so it was *our* piece of shit. Ham stared up at the thing, probably remembering the mess of a linoleum desert the Thank You, Texas Tour had to put up with, and gritted out his orders. The damned thing had *better* be made right, so git to it!

The Texas-shaped stage wasn't any better. Some Yankees must have made the damned thing, because a plywood toolshed floor at a heavy construction site would have looked more like the state of Texas. The whole thing had to be redone from end to end. The screaming of electric saws and drills began now, added to the general hysteria that filled the Astro Arena around the clock.

And then there was the matter of the animals. The platforms for the longhorn and the buffalo would have been comical if they hadn't cost so much. They served their intended purposes; they could hold the hundreds of pounds of animal with no problem. But they were made of solid iron, and consisted of more pieces than a retirement home jigsaw puzzle. At the place where the contraptions had been fabricated, the welders had recognized that there might be difficulties with the multitude of parts, so to be helpful, each had been labeled for quick and *easy* assembly. Trouble was, there was no schematic provided, just a listing of parts and what each was supposed to hook onto. The parts weren't even named in a fashion that would be understandable outside an engineering lab: What in the hell does "part XB-2Y" mean to you, or me, or anybody? I could see that *quick*, *easy*, and *efficient* were words that would *never* be associated with this tour. We had a three-dimensional iron Rubik's Cube on our hands and some-times on our smashed toes.

The steer and buffalo which were to mount these platforms had been corraled at a ranch outside Houston, where they were subjected daily to hours of blaring rock and roll music for beast-conditioning. When we finally got the platforms together near the end of rehearsal week, they were trucked in and tested out on top of their pig-iron pedestals. There were still some worries that the big animals might wig out when confronted with the thundering noise of a real rock concert, even if sedated, so a rented security guard was set to work by Ham to give them further conditioning. This guy would sneak up underneath the platforms at irregular intervals and squeeze off a few shots with a blank gun. Standing under a platform that supported a half-ton, well-fed bovine, and trying to intentionally spook it, required more courage (or less intelligence) than I would ever have mustered. The steer and buf-falo eventually got so they would put up with anything. Either they were now conditioned or they had gone stone deaf.

Parked inside in the middle of everything were one of four semitrailers, getting a custom-paint job in sequence. Three of them were going to be painted with a scenic panorama of Texas, and the fourth would have the tour logo. The last would take the lead on the road and act as flagship for the fleet. Lined up end to end at the shows, they would make an impressive mural/adver-tisement almost two hundred feet long.

The madness of construction got down to the last two days, and things were enough together so that it seemed like a good time for the band to actually play a few tunes surrounded by their new toys. Climb in there, Boys, and take 'er for a spin around the block! Kick those tires! (Not too hard.) Slam those doors! (Take it easy.) Admire your reflections in the paint job! (We're working on getting it shiny.)

Most people have the misconception that "rehearse" means to go through an entire show song by song, so that musicians and crew can work out all the lighting, effects, choreography, and whatnot. With Bill Ham, "rehearse" meant playing ten seconds of the opening and closing songs around seventy or eighty times apiece, on the theory that these are the most important (maybe the *only* important) songs in a gig, as they set and wind up the mood of the audience. Ham was determined that whatever the hell else went wrong with the tour, ZZ Top would at least start and finish each show right.

Hearing only a few bars of "Thunderbird" over and over again was totally maddening. The only pleasure we got out of it was taken from watching the expressions of the hundred-plus "friends" of ZZ Top who had showed up to eyeball the road show—for free. They thought they were going to see a sneak *preview* of the new show. Instead, they got a sneak *attack* on their nervous systems and hearing, couched in a Keystone Kops routine.

Somewhere along the way, Ham had a stroke of brilliant inspiration. The whole world knew that ZZ Top was produced by Lone Wolf Productions, whose logo was a howling wolf. What about getting a live wolf to perch in the middle of the stage while ZZ was being introduced? And what about getting the wolf to pose in full howling mode, too? He contacted Ralph Fisher, the animal trainer, and asked him about it. Fisher informed Ham that finding a wolf to train wouldn't be much trouble, but imagining that anyone could get it to pose in front of tens of thousands of screaming fans on a nightly basis amounted to a triumph of hope over reality.

Fisher suggested an alternative: He would "make up" a German shepherd to *look* like a wolf. Yeah, a shepherd. Dogs are domesticated, after all, and a lot easier to train than their wild cousins. He came up with a mongrel from somewhere, and Ham laid on our old friend Bill Narum, the artist, to handle the canine makeover. He and Fisher tried to spray paint this hound to look like a northern timber wolf. The result was as bad as that linoleum desert Ham claimed we had desecrated. The mutt looked like an anorexic coyote hooked on Grecian Formula. So much for that.

It did provide a humorous memory, though. For a few passes on the perpetual "Thunderbird" loop, Ralph Fisher tried out hiding behind our eight-foot-square Lone Wolf logo, trying to entice the gene-deficient shepherd to raise its head into howling mode by dangling a piece of cheese in front of his nose on the end of a bent coat hanger. The only howls he evoked for his efforts were from the audience and the crew.

The live wolf didn't work out, so Bill Ham thought up an alternative. He got a tape recording of a wolf howling its heart out for the sound engineer to play when the show was about to start, then had us rehearse *that* along with "Thunderbird" about fifty times. By the end, with all that howlin' and short-shuffle boogie, we were so mentally and physically whacked we had developed a cross-eyed stupor. *"Howoooooooo . . . ! Ka-thump a thump a thump a thump a thump a thump a Git high, everybody! Git high . . . !"* It drove away the last remnants of the short-change preview audience, and nearly the crew with them.

Finally it was all over. We were ready to roll, and wrapped things up in the arena. Ham left. The Boys left. And after loading all the equipment and staging, the roadies left, too. The last big push, to get the heck out of the arena before we hit overage and the clock started ticking penalty money, had lasted no less than forty-six hours straight. We were so beat we had to drive in shifts to make it home, even though we all lived less than twenty minutes away.

A few days afterward the tour was born.

When everybody started showing up at the embarkation point, many strange faces were seen in the crowd. It seemed as though somebody had hired a few extra "technicians" without letting the regular crew in on it. The Old Guard roadies loaded into one bus, the strangers into the other. There was so much confusion coming down that anybody who showed up could have gone on tour with us and not been spotted for days. "Say, Dave, who's that guy over there standing next to the buffalo?" "Beats me. I thought he was working with *you!*" The way things turned out, it actually wouldn't have been bad to have a few stowaways to con into doing some work for us.

A couple of days later we arrived in Winston-Salem, North Carolina, for the kickoff of the World-Wide Texas Tour. It was to be an *outdoor* show. Nice touch. We had barely been able to build this sumbitch *indoors* one time before, and now here we were about to do it in the breeze. Slick—that's all I can say. Slick.

Things looked even better when the local, typically excessive fans began to pull their tricks. First, two knife-wielding Hell's Angels cleared a swath right there in the middle of 25,000 concertgoers. Then some local bikers and a contingent of Marines entered into philosophical debate over some moot point of etiquette. As I watched the ambulance hauling away the losing debaters, I hoped it wasn't an indicator of things yet to come. Unfortunately, it was.

A set change ought to take thirty to forty-five minutes. The one we did before the WWTT show got going took an hour and a half, mainly because it had never all been put together in a single, unified effort. People were running around bumping into each other like insurance salesmen at a quintuplet birth. One little problem that developed first was our old outdoor nemesis, wind. When the drops to the 3D panorama were unfurled, the result was creation of a spinnaker sail a quantum jump bigger than anything Dennis Conner ever hoisted at a defense of the America's Cup. The wind was about to take the voluminous backdrop and a part of the stage off to New Zealand in a hurry. Common sense finally prevailed. We brought the thing back under control and wrote it off for this particular show.

It didn't matter anyway. The audience that had survived the biker-biker and bikers-Marines getdowns couldn't have cared less about refinements of production theory. They just wanted to boogie. At an outdoor show, volume is all that really matters. If a band can produce sound that peels flesh off skulls in the first ten

141

rows or provides justification for environmental impact research in a five-mile radius, the fans will be left ecstatic.

The steer and the buffalo were raised and presented to a crowd that had no idea what in the hell it was all about. About the only production effect that caused a ripple of interest was Frank's dismantling of his entire new drum set during the first song and replacing it with his old one. ZZ Top played this lead gig LOUD. Thirty-five thousand Carolinians went home happy. That was all there was to it.

After the show was over and the temporary musical fantasy had ended, cold reality gripped the ZZ crew in a stranglehold. It was time for the dreaded load-out. We looked forlornly at the scattered masses (I should say "messes") of some fifty tons of equipment (one labeled XB-2Y) which we were responsible for putting back in the trucks in such a way that it could be reassembled with ease at the next concert. The task just didn't seem humanly possible. Still, we had to try.

The normal time to load after an outdoor show, not counting the stage, is roughly five or six hours. *Fourteen* hours after it was born—at 2:00 P.M. the next day—the WWTT was finally loaded up and ready to roll. The show's parents were in a hotel resting comfortably, and the *doctors* were on life support systems. But it had been done. This cross-breeched, ass-over-tea kettle, butthole son of a technical bitch was delivered and on its way in the world. Nothing could stop us now.

Except maybe Scope Arena in Norfolk, Virginia, the next gig. This place is the worst venue (from a crew standpoint) in the United States, next to Boston Garden. Scope's situation necessitated pushing all the equipment—all fifty tons of it—a couple of hundred yards from trucks to the stage. It seemed like the job would never end, and in fact at 9:30 A.M. the morning after we had started, the local union boss was forced to call in a swing shift to finish the ZZ Top load-out. These guys finished up at 11:30 A.M., making total time to set up, perform, and reload no less than twenty-seven hours. The record for longest consecutive outdoor and indoor load-outs had been set. Hope somebody alerted the *Guinness Book of Records* people about it. I didn't. I was crashed, burned, and buried.

From these dubious origins, and once a few shows had been gotten behind us, the *enfant terrible* tour was more under control. The attending physicians provided needed therapy and surgery, including excising the cancerous tumor of the animal platforms. Good-bye piece number XB-2Y! These were replaced with modern, portable versions that worked much more efficiently and didn't have to be torn apart and reassembled all the time. It was clear that our child would never exactly run, but at least now it could crawl and toddle.

Following are vignettes that encapsulate the essence of the ZZ Top World-Wide Texas Tour.

At the Sugar Bowl in New Orleans, during setup the day before the show, the buffalo managed to escape. Perhaps it was the prospect of another session of Texas Boogie, perhaps he just saw his chance to break for freedom, but suddenly Tex yanked free from his handler and took off at full gallop. Don Fox, the promoter of the show, happened to be standing near at hand in all his 250 pounds of meat and bone. As the buffalo rushed past, Fox turned on the juice and thundered off after him, trying somehow to bring things under control. What a sight it made: two massive beasts hurtling along in a symphony of natural grace and beauty. If you squinted, it was hard to tell which of the hurtling animals should be brought down first if matters got dangerous and they had to be shot.

Ralph Fisher finally corralled the buffalo. To this day Don Fox still runs free.

At an outdoor show in Nashville, the longhorn, Texas, played the same trick on us as the buffalo. He got loose at a racetrack *during* the show. One second Texas was mulling over Nietzsche, the next he had flatfoot leaped right out of his six-foot-high pen. The ZZ crew spent about three hours running back and forth along the racetrack, trying to haze our beef away from the ogling crowd and the inevitable injuries and lawsuits that would ensue if he got loose among the Tennesseans. With the aid of some instantaneously deputized wranglers we were able to keep the steer contained in the backstage area. Texas would break for a gap. The gap would fill with yelling Texans and Tennesseans. Texas would spin and haul ass somewhere else, only to be stopped in the same way. Some of the backstage guests treated it like a New World running of the bulls in Pamplona, Spain.

Ralph Fisher was the one who got Texas penned, just as he had Tex, but it had taken three hours of sprinting here and there by all of us to get the job done. Not only did it cause me to miss one of the Band's last performances, I was so tired I could barely call cues for ZZ Top's show. I made a point of having steak for my next meal so I could pretend it was that damned longhorn. Judging by my sirloin's taste and toughness, it very well could have been.

It was one of the buzzards' turns to provide a little adventure when we got to Washington, D.C. ZZ was playing the Capitol Center, which has a video system that projects immense images on four big screens hung at arena center. Naturally we wanted everything to look its best here in the nation's capital, so additional steps were taken to ensure this.

The buzzard, which as usual was tethered to a perch just behind Dusty's speaker stacks, proved to be a great instinctive showman. Whenever a white spotlight was trained on him he would unfold his wings to maximum, a six-foot span. This was pretty dramatic every time he did it, so we decided to feature him for the video. A crewman was detailed to put a light a few feet away from the buzzard so that he could be illuminated from below as well as from above to enhance the video footage, and we forgot about it for the moment. It was time for liftoff of the show.

A bare three songs into the performance, Ralph Fisher came sprinting over to my side of the stage and whispered something into the ear of Bobby Gordon, the lighting technician who was on headsets with me. Bobby waited for his break in the cue-calling, and then spoke. "Dave, Ralph says you're frying his buzzard." It was in calm deadpan, as if he was discussing nuclear proliferation or a balm for athlete's foot.

I looked over at the perch. The helpless buzzard was dangling upside down, hanging by his tethered leg, weakly flapping his wings, tongue hanging out of his beak, puking his guts out. The light that somebody had set up three feet away for the bird's up-lighting was a 750-watt Leko *spotlight*, which produces a very concentrated beam. Evidently it had been left on since the show had started. The poor buzzard's feathers were actually smoking. WE WERE MICROWAVING THAT POOR SUCKER ALIVE!

There was a strangled, gasping sound from the audience. One of the crew was pointing at the video screens. I looked, and up there in a video projection twenty feet high the buzzard was getting his literal place in the sun before God and man. ZZ Top was getting known for its unusual sets, but this was something really new, all right. No audience had ever seen a special effect in which a live buzzard was rotisserie-broiled for their rock and roll pleasure.

"Gawd Almighty!" somebody yelled. "Boy, turn off that bird's spotlight before we have to bury him in a Col. Sanders bucket!" Suddenly we were all laughing our asses off at the plight of the buzzard, and at what the crowd must be thinking about our special effects budget. "Jesus! ZZ Top's gonna be hittin' sixty cities. You don't think they'll incinerate a buzzard for every show, do you?"

145

We got the light turned off and the buzzard cooled down before he could burst into flames. After he got a little water in him and on him he stopped smoldering and was able to sit up, blinking and coughing. Then he was able to go on and finish the tour. What a trouper.

At least, I *think* he did. Ralph some time later mentioned that the names of his buzzards were Oscar I, Oscar II, and Oscar IV (a creative stroke suggesting the genius behind the names of Texas and Tex). What happened to Oscar III? I never asked, and I don't think I really want to know. But for the next few years, every time I ate chicken, I thought about it.

By the time WWTT got back to Houston, it was pretty much organized and functional. Most of the problems of infancy had been overcome; just about everybody had something good to say about the thing, about how sharp and cute it was. That was good. It was time to channel all energies into achieving a perfect show in our hometown of Houston.

When a band plays its hometown, every effort is made to make sure that not only is the act's shit together, it can lift it as well. After all, Aunt Pearl, cousin Eustice, nephew Dicky Don, and a whole slew of friends, neighbors, and distant relatives not heard from in years are going to hit you up for those much-coveted backstage passes. When they find out that all you can give them are ordinary tickets out front, where they must sit with the ordinary mortals, you've got to make it up to them by delivering your best show. If you fail, forget Christmas cards and invitations to family reunions. You'll be disowned by them all.

ZZ's hometown gig was to be at the Summit, an indoor arena given its name, I expect, because it's way up there on a twenty-foot-high salt dome bubble—about as much mountain as you get on the Gulf Coast plain. The Summit also has a video system, just like in Washington. Great pains were being taken with the lighting of Oscar (I, II, or IV?) so as not to set him sizzlin' this time. I requested that my cueing headset system be tied in with the video booth so that the video director could be given precise notice where to focus next. This would tighten the lighting and video and make for an improved overall presentation.

As hoped, everything was moving along in great style and serious technical ass was being kicked. The opening act and set change ran ahead of schedule. It was the start of a storybook triumph for ZZ Top back on the old stomping grounds. The mayor had declared it "ZZ Top Day" and given the band the key to the city. The sky boxes at the Summit were packed with glittering local luminaries, such as the Mayor, several city councilmen, administrators from the University of Houston, various social movers and shakers. And, as the great occasion justly deserved, the Summit was also graced by all of their lovely wives. Who would ever have thought, back in 1969, that it would ever come to this? Here ZZ Top had a truly triumphant return.

The Summit is ordinarily used for sporting occasions, especially basketball onslaughts by the Rockets against all comers. The house camera crew frequently stirred up some energy during slack sporting events, or set changes at rock concerts, by using the fancy video system to project images of attractive females in the crowd. A few good "honey" shots generally did the trick, especially since there was always a roar from the crowd for the girl on the screen to "show some skin," which translated into flashing her tits. Some didn't, most did, while still other lovelies would elect to show a lot more than that. Video flashing was a great, truly Texan means of crowd control. This was a giant leap from the red hot mamas stripping at the old cellar clubs.

Therefore it is no small wonder that during the set change, and after I finished briefing the spotlight operators, I made a quip for the ages. Because of those great X-rated moments served up in the Summit by local femme fatales, I told the guys to ". . . sit back, relax, and check out all the *fine* pussy." I followed that advice myself. I stood back, stretched, and laced fingers behind my head. The ZZ Top homecoming was headed for in-the-bag perfect.

But what was this? Several people were running toward the stage, in fact headed straight toward *me*. What the . . . ? The first to puff up was Bobby Gordon, my headset compadre and engineer. He answered my questioning look by relaying the scintillating news flash that in order for my cues to be piped into the video booth it had required pegging into the V.I.P. skybox system. As a result, I had just given explicit instructions to the *creme de la creme* of Houston society to hang loose and watch for boobs and beavers!

Even though I later heard a rumor that some of the wives of the skybox dignitaries actually wet their pants laughing at my *faux pas*, the embarrassment of that moment lingers with me to the present day.

A few months later the ZZ Top World-Wide Texas Tour came to a conclusion. They didn't know it yet, but Billy, Dusty, and Frank were about to start a much-deserved break. The longhorn and the buffalo were put back out to pasture; the rattlesnakes went back to the snake house; the buzzards went back to Ralph Fisher's aviary. All that was left of the WWTT adventure was a warehouse full of surplused leftover gear. All was well with the world.

All was well on the financial front, too. The ZZ Top World-Wide Tour was reported to have grossed over $11,000,000, a record at the time. Even after you subtracted out the huge sums that it had taken to give birth to the tour, nurture it, and carry it along, there was still a lot left over for Ham and the Boys. And the band's profile had never been higher.

The phenomenal success of WWTT meant that recording sales would keep on booming long after the last tremors from the tour agitated accountants, the IRS, or any of the other Powers That Be. Bill Ham had done it. He had carried out his promise to make Billy Gibbons a star, and along the way had done the same thing for Dusty Hill and Frank Beard. Now they were all rich, just as he had said they would be back in the beginning.

And of course, so was he.

10

TURNIN' THE CORNER

Hysterical pregnancy—there's the perfect analogy to describe the first megatouring efforts of ZZ Top. I prefer this use of words instead of *total insanity* because although everybody from the band down to the lowest roadie felt nuts before, during, and after each and every one, these tours developed an inertial drive that picked up and carried everybody and everything along with it like a natural, inexorable force. After the ZZ Top World-Wide Texas Tour was finished, we found that for all its agonies and ecstasies it had also been one hell of a training and proving ground on the theory and practice of lofting big shows. Once you've lived through a hysterical tour or two, I guess it gets to be second nature to just "spit those suckers out."

While designing tours got easier with practice for the ZZ Top circus, it never did become anything near scientific. It was always pure art from start to finish. Sometimes things started with a tour concept and music was built around it; sometimes things started with some music and the tour was generated almost accidentally. Frank once laughed during an interview and gave me a facetious compliment. "Actually," he said, "the light show is the show. The music is just a background for the lights!"

This was one of the truly fun things about being involved in the creation of a rock and roll production. You could get bleeding-eyes high or snot-slinging drunk, and through veils of chemical creativity come up with the most outlandish ideas conceivable. Then, incredibly, somebody else would foot the bills so that your dreams, fantasies, or for that matter paranoid schizophrenic delusions could become a reality on stage. Why, I've even heard of some people designing a production while they were *straight*! Not me; that was too much like working a high-wire act with no net.

The ZZ Top rock and roll rodeo factory had about three years in which to develop its next production after WWTT. I can assure you that merely having a longer gestation period does *not* make eventual delivery any easier.

The reason why ZZ had such a long break in the action (1976 to 1979) was because Bill Ham was in the process of switching record labels. Back in 1970, when Ham had first signed ZZ with London Records, it was the hottest company going. But by the time the World-Wide Texas Tour came to an end, things had changed. The aging London Records moguls had lost a lot of their punch and savvy, and most of their rock acts. Their stable, which once had included the Rolling Stones and the Moody Blues (I wonder if they ever played Española), was almost empty. It was time for ZZ Top to vacate what was left of the premises before somebody had the band shoveling out the musical stalls.

I think the final corporate straw that broke Ham's management back dropped when London released the *Best of ZZ Top* album in 1977. London high-handedly stomped on Ham's ego (and probably his contractual rights) by leaving him almost entirely out of the process of album construction. He was virtually excluded from approval on selection of songs, order of presentation, or even cover artwork. London just cranked it out to fulfill ZZ's contractual obligations, which had included the usual clause on the number of albums to be released within a given period of time. So far the band had put out *ZZ Top's First Album* (1970), *Rio Grande Mud* (1972), *Tres Hombres* (1973), *Fandango* (1975), and *Tejas* (1976). Apparently, as far as Ham was concerned, the undiscussed retrospective album made it six and good-bye.

Bill Ham was as subtle and shrewd a businessman as he was ruthless. Although he was steamed about the "greatest hits" bit, he never let on or raised much of a stink about it. This was so that he could have the last laugh later. When ZZ left London, Ham arranged it so that he could take the entire ZZ Top record catalog along, too. It was an almost unbelievable coup, maybe the first in rock and roll history. Compare it to a bank president resigning his position, then moseying out the front door with all the deposits with the staff applauding. Ham was as good as they come.

Having gotten off the fat, flatulent London horse, it was now time to come up with a snorting, pawing charger. Ham started shopping around immediately, but without any particular sense of urgency. The Boys were hot stuff, the old albums were still selling, and the money was plentiful, even if no tours were underway. And with all the previous ZZ Top songs under his arm he had some heavy-duty clout on the negotiations front.

I can imagine how the phone calls went.

"Hello, Warner Brothers? This is Bill Ham down at Lone Wolf in Houston. I'm fine, thanky. Listen, I'm phonin' to see if y'all might be interested in signing an established, major profile rock and roll band with the rights to all six of its previous albums, some gold and some going platinum. . . . No sir, that's no bullshit, mister! And the band is ZZ Top. . . . Why sure, they're writin' up new material all the time, boy. . . . Well, hot damn! Get back to me on that one, junior. We'll do lunch, and maybe somebody's little sister, too! Ha!"

Undoubtedly possession of the catalog was the *big* selling point as negotiations moved ahead. After Ham did lunches here and there around the globe, twitching that bait around under the noses of one record company after another (like Ralph Fisher's coat hanger full of cheese), he finally settled on a deal. Warner Brothers did indeed become ZZ Top's new home in 1978.

Meanwhile, back at the ranch, the Boys were getting a little restless. About the only thing they were accomplishing was letting their beards grow. I'm not sure if it was a cohesive decision, or if they had all gotten too lazy to shave, but all three began to cultivate chin growths. They were tired of not working—loafing gets to be hard on you after a year or two of it—and wanted to get back on the road. It was where they felt the best. All the inactivity had been tough on the waistlines, especially Dusty's. He was getting tired of Ham threatening him with banishment to a fat farm before his "stage persona" would be deemed acceptable. On the up side, Frank had decided that if he wanted to live to age thirty-five he'd better get that drug gorilla of his bucked off, so he was using the time to dry out, air out, and cool out. As for Billy, he was mainly getting writer's cramp from writing up gag postcards to be mailed from faraway lands he might or might not have visited. He was known to have handed piles of them to travelling friends so that recipients back home could find cards from him in their mailboxes simultaneously sent from Katmandu and Upper Volta. You never really knew with Billy. He *might* be off somewhere, after all. It helped add pleasant confusion and "mystique" to Billy's image.

"Mystique" was Bill Ham's favorite buzzword at this point in time. ZZ Top had been perfunctorily going through the motions of rehearsal over the months. Nothing regular, you understand, but there was no hurry. Nevertheless, out of these sessions had come some new tunes that appeared to be keepers. The Boys were aware that their first album for Warner had to be better than average to cement the relationship securely. The music played easy and smooth, and they were confident that it would do the trick. At this point, the only real problem was that they weren't gigging, and it made them a little edgy.

Out of boredom, Billy the gagster dreamed up something to pass an afternoon or two. He talked Dusty and Frank into shooting a publicity photo of the three of them dressed up as a fictitious band. From a costume shop he rented tuxedos and red berets; a musical instrument store provided three saxophones. As a final touch, Billy bought three pairs of white gloves and black shades. Then it was off to the photographer's for a picture of ZZ Top posed with the instruments like some 1960's horn section in a rhythm and blues review. Once the pictures were developed, he sent the so-called publicity photo to Bill Ham with a note attached saying, "Bill—please try to find some work for these guys. Billy." At the bottom of the picture was Billy's name for the mythical group: "The Lone Wolf Horns."

Everybody in Bill Ham's office had a good chuckle the day the gag picture arrived in the mail. "Boy, that's Billy for you. Always has something new and unique to lay on you." It was a pretty good brainstorm, all right. What none of them knew was that in just the short time it had taken for the picture to travel from Billy's hands to Ham's, the Lone Wolf Horns had actually started to draw breath. The Boys heard that Robert DeNiro had learned to play sax for his role in *New York, New York* in a very short time. All three had seen the movie and agreed that his playing was very passable. That got them to thinking. Hell, if an *actor* could learn how to play the sax, certainly true *musicians* could really make a horn blow!

From the thought to action took only a phone call lining up some saxophone lessons. They had all the stuff used in the gag photo ready for use when the time came, and sat down to write up some new music. After several days of intensive practicing, the Boys could play their saxophones well enough to integrate them into two songs, "Hi Fi Mama" and "She Don't Love Me, She Loves My Automobile." In truth, "well enough" as a descriptive term for ZZ's saxophone competence encompasses varying degrees of total ineptitude ranging from "shitty" to "sucks," but somehow the songs actually worked.

154

Pete and I acted as sound engineers so that Billy, Dusty, and Frank could tape guitar, bass, and drum parts down in the storage warehouse, a building that doubled as a minimum-budget rehearsal facility. This tape provided the backup for their sax playing. When they felt that they were ready, the Boys invited Bill Ham to come down and listen to some new material. The sax lessons had been kept a secret, so Ham just thought he was going to hear some normal ZZ Top boogie. There was no reason to expect anything out of the ordinary.

When Ham arrived, the Boys stayed out of sight. He was directed to a strategically located chair, where he sat down slightly amused by all the mystery but fully aware that "artists are funny, boy." After a dramatic pause, the instrumental tracks for the first horn tune were fed through the warehouse sound system. As the music started, Billy, Dusty, and Frank appeared, and Ham's jaw dropped. The Boys were truly resplendent in their Lone Wolf Horns regalia of tuxedos, red berets, white gloves, and impenetrable shades. By this time their beards had begun to bloom, so they looked like Amish/French pimps on their way to a beef and bird soiree. And the music was something else. Backed by their recorded selves, the three musicians did the sax parts live. Although some of the horn notes came out sounding like the north ends of southbound Canadian honkers, it wasn't bad after a few short lessons and minimal practice. And to top it off, the Boys had thrown in some horn section choreography á la James Brown's Famous Flames.

Bill Ham was absolutely delighted with the whole bit. It had come out of nowhere, it didn't fit with any part of the Boys' image to that point, but the Lone Wolf Horns was material to work with, all right. There was just something so lunatic about the way Billy, Dusty, and Frank looked in those costumes, the gag photo come to life—sequin-spangled ZZ Top flipped into reverse-field blackface. A revised concept of what ZZ Top could become was stirring in Ham's canny mind, something to stir up the fans all over again, bigger and better than ever.

The Boys had always been known for their no-holds-barred style of music. They were about to become known for a no-holds-barred image. You can see what I mean if you examine the first Warner album, *Deguello,* with close attention.

When it came out in 1979, the artwork of the album alone was mind-blowing. It presented a smashed human skull with smoke wafting up out of the eye sockets under a white flag of truce, and apparently being blown to smithereens by the Forces of Darkness. Both the cover and the title were Ham's way of re-orienting ZZ Top's persona. For those of you out there who don't know much Texas history, "Deguello" was the bugle call signal-ling "no quarter" which Santa Ana's army played the morning it overran the Alamo and butchered Crockett, Bowie, and several dozen other abandoned heroes of the Texas Revolution. To Ham, the squashed-skull cover was supposed to symbolize somebody's ass getting kicked while trying to peacefully surrender, thus "no quarter" was being given. As he traced out his meandering logic, the "somebody" came to be ZZ Top's audiences, then the record industry. Oh! Now I get it. And when you removed the inner liner, there were the Lone Wolf Horns with their tuxes, berets, saxes, and shades.

Hmmmm. A play on the period attire worn during the de-fense of the Alamo, perhaps? Or is it deeper than that? Heavy, man. I'm in deep need of some vapor therapy. Pass the leaf.

That cover came off about as comprehensibly as a Grateful Dead's Greatest Flops ensemble. A lot of confused fans and gulli-ble Warner executives may have gotten it, but I sure didn't. I thought it was just a bunch of crosswired bullshit. Which helped to explain why efforts to put together a tour concept to go with the album required no small amount of contemplation as we all grasped at straws.

Here's where the spontaneous wit and innovative powers of yours truly came into the picture. I was performing the functions of both production and lighting designer by now and I decided to seize the opportunity to demonstrate my great worth to ZZ Top by exercising imagination at full wattage. It's one thing to think up one production worth of ideas—in fact, that's the easy part. All you have to do is get high as a kite on your mind-altering chemicals of choice and let your brain aimlessly fumble around inside your skull like a blind liberal in a voting booth. Something is bound to come out of the kaleidoscope, hopefully scribbled down on the back of a cocktail napkin or billing envelope before you pass out. No sir, the *real* talent is to get that special somebody to have enough faith in your ideas to slap down enough gift wrap to pay for them.

Mainly because nobody—not Ham, not the Boys, *nobody*— had a clear idea what to do with the tour concept problem, I ventured some basic suggestions. Suddenly, and I'm not quite sure how the scenario unfolded, they tossed the responsibility for the whole *Deguello* production design into my lap. I had done the lighting designs for all the prior tours, but the production designs had usually been fulminated out of a mishmash of ideas popped out by everybody. This would be my first time doing the works. Why not? There had to be an easier way than the chaotic, tangle-footed approach that was our hallmark in the past.

I started with the stage itself. I wanted it to be lighted, but also provide constant tone instead of the "hot spots" inherent in the period's basic disco stage. The stage should also be set up so that I could use its features to perform special wild effects essentially under the feet of the performers. Before long it all began to seem overwhelming. In the course of puzzling over my notes and drawings, I decided that it was obvious I needed some outside help, so I went and got it.

With the help of Jim Moody at Sundance Lighting I got in touch with an old geezer in Las Vegas by the name of Fred Way, an expert in fiber optics. I suppose you could call him *the* expert, since he and Salvador Dali *invented* fiber optics for the World's Fair in 1960. Fred said that he would be happy to help, and together we designed a fiber-optic stage on which you could produce solid colors, colored geometric designs, musical symbols, firework bursts, and moving vortexes of rainbows. It was a one-of-a-kind stage, both more impressive and cheaper than what had gone into the WWTT follies. At $40,000 it was a bargain, and Ham agreed to have the thing built. To implement this fabulous creation for the audiences down in front, I had a sixteen-by-forty-foot Mylar reflector fabricated to hang at the rear of the set. Its height and angle could be adjusted to fit each venue's sighting requirements and would give a clear overhead look at the stage and the performers.

From the first time I saw the Boys doing their sax thing down in the warehouse, I *knew* that the Lone Wolf Horns would have to be part of the *Deguello* show. Billy and I started talking it over even before the sax tunes were formally included in the album. We agreed that employing three genuine sax players dressed up like the Lone Wolves had to be ruled out immediately. It had to be the real McCoys, or in this case the real ZZ Boys, or nothing. Since the band couldn't be in two places at once, that left projecting an image of the Lone Wolves behind the stage where ZZ was playing and letting the sound track of the filmed Boys tool along with the actual Boys below. Video would be easier, but no way was Bill Ham going to spring for the expense of a delicate video projector. So the final and most cost-effective option was 16 millimeter film. It all seemed pretty simple to me.

Billy didn't see it that way. He was concerned about synchronizing live music with the film's music and he wasn't sure how to reproduce the saxophone sounds faithfully. Moreover, what if the film broke, as films frequently did? That would leave ZZ on stage trying to play guitars and saxes at the same time—quite a trick. The solution Billy came up with was to have the film run without a music soundtrack. The saxophones would be generated from a bastardized, poor man's sax synthesizer Billy designed using an eight-track tape machine and a small electric keyboard. Using them, a technician could play the sax notes as required. If the film did break in mid-song, the horn parts would still be there even after the Lone Wolf Horns had flashed into celluloid oblivion.

That did the trick. So for all but a few performances, when Billy's guitar tech Jimmy Emerson switched in, Pete Tickle was the unseen fourth Lone Wolf Horn adding in the syntho-sax sounds.

Now to make the film. Billy and I scouted locations for the outdoor shots in his lowrider Chevy. This was a car he had lately picked up as the West Coast lowrider craze got underway; as usual he had dived into the scene head first. This "Chebby" had come equipped with power shocks that enabled the driver to raise or lower the front or rear end instantaneously. Billy naturally had to take this one step further by having remote controls installed. He could park the car and take the remote with him to play pranks.

As we drove along, Billy told me about how he had once parked the car in a no-parking zone in Austin. Across the street he hid inside a store, watching through the front window for a cop to spot the violation. It didn't take long. Along came one of Austin's infamous meter readers with a sheaf of tickets, ready to make some more money for the city from the short-time parking meters and scads of no-parking areas around town. When the meter reader reached over to put the ticket under a windshield wiper, Billy made the empty car jump up on its shocks like a goosed cat. The meter reader leaped back as if he'd been shocked. He furtively glanced around to see whether anyone else had seen the car buck. No one was near. Turning back, he made another grasp for the windshield wiper, and this time Billy hit the controls and the car hunkered down close to the ground. The rattled cop grinned weakly, wadded up the ticket, and left in defeat. The forces of the Twilight Zone were clearly present around that car, and there was no point in fighting them.

After cruising Houston for a while, popping the shocks up and down and scaring the wits out of unsuspecting drivers who stopped next to us at lights, Billy and I at last found the location we wanted. A local video and film company was contracted for the "shoot" and in a few days ZZ Top had its Lone Wolves sequence in the can.

Everything was coming together with unusual smoothness.

The elements of the *Deguello* production were now completed and potentially astounding, if consistent with the incomprehensible overall theme. We trucked the works over to Shreveport, Louisiana, for a dry run in the Coliseum. Memories of the Astro Arena were still too painful for a return there—some things never change. Just as with the World-Wide Texas Tour, we found ourselves doing more building than rehearsing. The fiber-optic stage was being wired literally until the instant ZZ Top walked onstage for their kick-off show, but miracle of miracles, it worked like a charm.

When the Boys hit the stage after a three-year layoff they were a little rusty and scared totally shitless. *They* didn't exactly work like charms, but they played with their customary intensity, and that compensated for all the musical screwups. The only problem that was really noticeable was Billy's eye makeup, which melted in the heat of the lights and ran down his cheeks as a bizarre ad lib. Prior to this, the Boys had scorned makeup on stage as being only for Kiss, but over the past three years, and especially under the influence of Ham's *Deguello* thinking, a lot of things had changed. ZZ Top had made a 180-degree turn from their neo-shit-kicker image to one of new wave/punk/yuppies. The stage show was no longer a barnyard review full of rural Texana. It was now a streamlined rock show full of special visual and musical effects.

The *Deguello* tour played to sold-out audiences across the United States and Canada. Clearly the hiatus as a new recording company was sought had not caused any fans to desert, and if anything the new ZZ look and sound helped recruit a few more. A hop across the Atlantic with the tour was made less for actual stage performances than for Bill Ham to get the Boys onto two important television shows—"The Olde Grey Whistle Test" in London, and "Rock Palast" in Essen, West Germany—which reached a vast viewership across Europe. "Rock Palast," a biannual multi-act event that on this occasion would reach an estimated 40 million people, was being legally broadcast for the first time in the former Soviet Union. Therefore, ZZ Top helped the world with a little rock and roll *peristroika* and *glasnost*. Who knows? ZZ Top might have triggered the end of Communism with this performance. The volume could have cracked the Berlin Wall.

The whole *Deguello* costuming and styling was ditched not long after the tour came to an end. Where the rest of it went I don't know, but as far as I know the fiber-optic stage is still sitting in a warehouse somewhere waiting to be used to its full potential. Because of the hyper-advanced qualities of the stage and the fact that the Boys were a step slower on the musical front, the stage might have had the edge when audiences tried to remember what they had witnessed.

In 1979 ZZ Top was ten years old, and *Deguello* was a whole lot different from what Billy, Dusty, and Frank had started off with. Of course, we were now all ten years older. Passing that miraculous dividing line—age thirty—does something to your head and your body. Somehow you start finding it harder to stay up all night rompin' stompin' drunk and tearing up hotel rooms. You actually want to have a place you live in, rather than a place you occasionally find your way back to for sleep. *Deguello,* now that I look back on it, was really sort of a remark about the confusion of finally finding yourself grown up but not being particularly happy about the discovery.

Yeah, *Deguello* was a successful album and a successful tour. But a corner had been turned and we all knew it. The good old days of struggle seemed a long time gone, something now to look back on a little wistfully.

The *El Loco* tour in 1981 put ZZ Top another two years farther down the road, and more things started to change. The Boys were still looking for something familiar yet progressive in both music and image. For *El Loco,* one big innovation being experimented with was for the Boys to start wearing some funky grease monkey coveralls in place of their usual fashion plate stage garb. Another was more extensive use of live "sound augmentation." They had done a little cheating of this sort on the *Deguello* tour on the song "Manic Mechanic" by adding in car sounds and dubs of Billy's voice.

Now ZZ Top was entering the new era of techno rock in a big way. The stage show incorporated synthesizer pumped through the sound system to help fill up ZZ's three-piece sound, and also to reproduce some of the parts on the album. But the fans didn't seem to notice or mind. Perhaps they were too busy staring at the stage set, this time designed by Tom Littrell, of Showco. It looked like space machinery straight out of *Alien*.

The final touch was the incorporation of a Vari-Lite system, which was a brand-new lighting innovation at the time. Genesis had helped fund the research and development of this invention, and when the new lighting system was finally ready, they took them out on their maiden tour. Now I was being given the privilege of using them.

Vari-Lite systems are computer-controlled lights that are programmed to instantly change color, aperture, and orientation at the touch of a button. You see them used today for stage lighting at most live concerts, in virtually all music videos, and in many movies and television shows. They make it possible to design dazzling lighting effects by creating and programming multitudes of beam movements in conjunction with instant aperture and color changes. They're the greatest innovation in rock and roll since somebody turned over a chain hoist and made it possible to hang sound, lights, and David Lee Roth from the venue ceiling.

This time when ZZ went to Europe, Bill Ham made up for lost time on the first trip by booking about twenty shows in twenty-five days. Because of the notoriety gained, especially from the Rock Palast gig during the *Deguello* tour, virtually all the shows were sold out, just like back in the States. The finale of this marathon was an appearance at London's Hammersmith Odeon on October 26, 1981, followed *thirty-six hours later* by a show with the Rolling Stones in the Astrodome! After that kind of power touring I literally had to take some R and R in the hospital to recuperate.

Just as they had in 1979 for *Deguello,* audiences came out in force for *El Loco.* Or were the audiences starting to be a little bit less numerous than they had been? Ham seemed to think so, and it appeared to worry him. ZZ Top might be losing its punch. That was unacceptable. Something would have to be done about it. Whether the golden goose needed some steroid shots, workouts in the gym, a deep enema, or a switch to decaf, Ham was going to make sure that he delivered.

In early 1983, after a little more than a year's break, it was time for another tour. This time the tour concept was the result of a lot more thought—perhaps I should say "balanced thought"—than its two immediate predecessors. Billy loved cars, and over several years' time had been having a custom hot rod built. Now the car was ready, and when he and Ham saw it they realized that this machine was just what punched the ticket for a tour theme. This car was destined for more than touring the country on the custom-car circuit, being ogled by blond-haired, blue-eyed, big-titted, beer-gutted, blue-collar bimbos with big butts and bad breath. This car was going to serve a much, much loftier purpose, namely fortifying and rebuilding ZZ Top.

If Billy and Ham played their cards right, they might be able to parlay a grease monkey look and that car into a device through which ZZ Top could make a bid for a musical market segment that up until now had been little touched by them. The type of people who frequented drag race ovals and hot-rod expositions generally favored country and western music. One reason was that they had been turned off when rock and roll was in its infancy by the look of the bands at the time. The Beatles in their 1963 pageboy haircuts and Edwardian suits look square today, but this gimmick was a big deal to contemporary rednecks. Despite the fact that a generation had passed and a lot of the country and western singers dressed and acted pretty wild, there was still a lot of resistance among their fans to anything smacking of rock and roll. What Billy and Ham wanted to do was to create a look and sound that would enlist the hot rodders of the United States into the ranks of ZZ Top fans.

To help with this project, Ham laid on the services of a guy named Mike Griffin. Mike had made a documentary film about the hot-rod scene called *Wheels on Fire* and knew his way around the drag race scene. His job description and title never really became too clear, but what he did was to serve as "technical advisor." He was a good guy, and turned out to be a good salesman to boot. A coup he helped to pull off which was most welcome was to help contract Schlitz as sponsor of the tour. When the tour concept was explained to the Schlitz executives, they quickly saw that if it worked as planned, blue-collar beer-swiggers would be paying attention to ZZ Top in an unprecedented way. Not only could a lot of beer be sold through sponsorships, the profile of the company's portfolio of beverages would be brought into sharp clarity through a relatively minor expenditure of promotional money.

Mike also contributed the album's name, albeit inadvertently. Ham had called a strategy meeting in his office one day prior to the startup of the tour. Pete, Mike, J. W. Williams, and I were there tying up loose ends before the tour got underway. Contrary to the way it is done in other production companies, Ham's method had usually been to get the Boys on the road, then follow along with the album later. Up until now this had been a big weak point, for a lot of album sales follow along in the wake of a tour — *if* they're available. Touring *prior* to an album's release is backwards. During the conversation the subject turned at one point to the as-yet untitled album, a burr under Ham's saddle which he needed removed pretty damned quick. It was highly unusual for Bill to ask for ideas on something this important, so when he solicited suggestions we enjoyed the opportunity to make a contribution.

164

Mike, in keeping with the hot rod theme, rolled over the first suggestion. "ZZ . . . Top Fuel?"

That got me thinking. "How about ZZ Top . . . Fuel?" I ventured.

Mike played with it a little more. "ZZ . . . Top Fuel Eliminator." When he saw Ham's puzzled face, he explained that Top Fuel Eliminator was hot rod jargon for a car that had gone through an elimination series of races to become the outright winner.

Ham leaned back in his chair, his lips pressed together. He thought out loud.

"ZZ Top . . . Eliminator. Eliminator. Eliminate the competition. That's it! We'll eliminate the competition." He obviously still had a few aggressive notions left over from *Deguello,* but in this case he was right on the mark. And so the name of a multi-platinum album was born.

Designing the stage show was old hat by now, at least once we had contacted every hydraulic lift company in the country and learned conclusively that it wasn't feasible to bring the Eliminator (as Billy's car was now named) along for posing on stage. Ham hadn't wanted the car up on a lift like the longhorn and buffalo; he wanted it to roll right up to the speaker stacks and drum set under its own power so that the Boys could make a real hot-rod entrance. This would have created all sorts of problems, however, not the least of which was reinforcement of performance stages to prevent the possibility of an unplanned mid-show elevator drop by the car. Use of a fiberglass model was ruled out, too, when it turned out that it would cost practically as much to build as the original. The solution was to have a replica of the album-cover car made up with movable headlights and the capacity to belch smoke and flame on command. It would be set up in front of a screen, on which would be projected a highway disappearing into the distance at a high rate of speed.

No production could get finished without Billy tossing in some suggestion that was off-the-wall. We were talking one night and he asked if we could have foam rubber mock-ups made of a lighting truss and some lights. When I asked him why, he said he wanted the show to end with everything seeming to fall apart. His inspiration took another leap. What about faking the demise of a spotlight operator, to go with it all? I liked that angle immediately. Several foam lights were made up easily enough over the next weeks, also a foam truss, a foam spotlight, and Billy's foam spotlight operator, who became known as Zeke. We didn't get around to a foam kitchen sink, but we had everything else.

Once the *Eliminator* tour got rolling, Billy's inspiration proved the high point of every show. At the end of the last bars of "Tush," the final encore song, there was the startling sound of an explosion up high. A section of truss would come falling down, followed by lights toppling one after the other; then the foam spotlight would drop off the real truss, followed by Zeke in all his glory. It was even arranged for Zeke to dangle by one hand for a moment before he plunged to his daily demise onstage. After he hit, a couple of the crew would run out on stage with a stretcher, put Zeke on it, and carry him off as if he were dead.

We finally had to stop doing this last part of the show because it looked so real that it was seriously upsetting a major part of the audience, only half-convinced up to then that it all was just a fake. People who were tripping on LSD. would stumble out after the show in hysterics, thinking that they had just witnessed a man die for the sake of rock and roll.

ZZ almost lost Zeke for real after the second show of the tour. Somebody stole the semi carrying the band gear and ransacked it. One of the few items left behind afterward was Zeke. I guess the thieves figured that foam men tell no tales. Billy lost some vintage guitars and a major portion of his amplifier array; Dusty lost some bass guitars; and I lost the full-sized foam rubber spotlight I had become very partial to. We also lost an expensive laser. Billy always pointed out when he told the story of the semi theft that they *took* everything in his wardrobe case and *left* everything in Dusty's.

Since there were four days until the next show on the tour,

we had time to pull off an all-time gear replacement coup. Back at the warehouse we dug out old amplifiers and speaker cabinets left over from tours back in the Mesozoic, and we even found some old guitars no one had thought about for a decade. The show was put back together in its entirety without missing a beat or a dollar from lost ticket sales. As we all learned at the Bill Ham Academy of the Entertainment Bidness, the show *always* goes on.

I mentioned before that ZZ Top was getting increasingly into the use of synthesizer assists after *Deguello*. *Eliminator* had synthesizer work in most of its songs, and so every song that was done live had the *exact* synth behind it, too. ZZ even had a live version of "TV Dinners" in which Dusty went through the motions of playing a synthesizer on stage while the *real* sound was on tape and being fed in by the sound crew. This was more cheating than they had ever done before, but what the hell? The show sounded better than it ever had and the audiences never complained. Why should they? The idea is to put on a performance and generate your unique sound for the audience's pleasure, and this is exactly what ZZ was doing—generating it. Like it or not, sound augmentation is here to stay.

Eliminator went over big. It even went to Europe, but I didn't go along. It was just prior to the last *Eliminator* show in the United States that I ran afoul of Bill Ham for the fourth and final time. Maybe I was making too much money to suit him—at least he started our parting conversation by informing me that he had cut my salary in half as of the previous week. I admit that there's always the chance that I might have lipped him once too often to suit his tastes. Whatever it was, he wanted to chop my income and I wouldn't work for what was left, so there you go. I decided to take a little vacation from show bidness, at least as it was navigated by Bill Ham.

Which is why I didn't see what went on with *Eliminator* in

Europe, with *Afterburner* in 1985, or with *Recycler* in 1990. I feel certain that they all were just extensions of what had been done previously. The music would continue to be techno, and judging from the albums, the stage sounds must have been great. The only thing I was ever curious about was what the lights looked like. Lights were always my first passion.

I had a couple of calls from Billy asking me to come back, that things could be patched up, but by then I had turned a new corner in life myself. Billy said that the lights just weren't the same without me, which was a compliment I value a great deal. But I was past thirty-five and that's too damned old for some people to be out there on the road. Come to think of it, fifteen years of roadie work is long enough to give to rock and roll, even with one of the best bands ever to come along. So I declined Billy's offer and wished him and the other guys good luck.

I've never looked back on my decision. All those years on the road had taken their toll and the old cost-to-benefit ratio was getting pretty problematic, despite the eventual healthy income.

Once you've been part of the circus, the bad times eventually become humorous anecdotes, and the good times seem to have been so much more fun than they really were. Because of the way I departed, there were no visits to the Lone Wolf offices anymore, and I didn't feel like I could drop in on the Boys. As time passed I noticed that I would sit up straight and read intently whenever some tidbit of ZZ Top news appeared in the papers, or look closely at any of their TV or video appearances. Even though I was into other things, I have to confess getting a bit wistful about the "good old days" once in a while.

Which made it inevitable, I suppose, that I would make one final meander back to the fold, perhaps thinking deep inside that maybe my current life was a dream, and the life with ZZ Top was still there, waiting to take me by the hand.

PART IV

RUNNIN'
ON

11

BACK TO THE FOLD . . . SORT OF

I t was early in 1990. One morning I read in the newspaper that ZZ Top, after several years of nothing but MTV appearances and reissues of old music, was returning to the rock and roll spotlight via a new album release and megatour. There it was: ZZ Top still lived after nearly twenty years, same three guys up onstage, same manager.

Not the same roadie ensemble, though. While some of the guys I had worked with backstage were still there—probably—*I* was history. The idea somehow seemed hard to take, and my coffee got cold while I thought about the band, the good old days, and how ordinary my life had become. More settled by far, no hazards, and the comfortable pleasures of hearth and home. But not filled with pranks and panics, adrenalin and airplanes, hijinks and wild stories. Mainly not with the music and the men who made it.

The tour for the new album, *Recycler*, got moving with the usual hype and cheers. Ham outdid himself laying the groundwork, complete with getting the Boys into doing the theme song for the movie *Back to the Future III* and making a cameo appearance in it. Soon I read that *Recycler* had made it up to number 6 on the *Billboard* charts, and that the tour was selling out at over one hundred stadiums, coliseums, and arenas around the country. Inevitably the weeks passed as new triumphs mounted, keys to cities were handed out, interviews were given . . . and the time for another homecoming back in Houston, once more at the Summit, got closer.

I decided I had to go see the show. After eight years away from it, the circus still beckoned.

The day of the performance—one of four Houston sell-out houses back-to-back—arrived and I found myself driving toward the Summit feeling some strange emotions. My heart actually beat faster the closer I got. My palms were sweating. I was like an ugly ingenue on opening night.

Hell, I thought indignantly. Time marches on. If the production is slicker than anything I helped design, what of it? New technology will always surpass the old. Who cares, and what's the big deal?

The big deal was fear of rejection.

What if the guys on the ZZ Top crew who had once been my close friends didn't remember me? Or recognize me, for that matter. The years whittle away at all things, after all. For all I knew, nobody from the old days was still there except for Billy, Dusty, Frank, and Bill Ham. What if there was no one left to answer my stage entrance pleas for admittance? I would have to sulk away into the shadows, forgotten, defeated, reduced to being just one of the masses of fans.

A fan? Me? The bane of the wolf, no less . . . to even think about it.

Memories haunted my mind—smoke from the explosions, laser effects dazzling the eyes, the music booming away. I seemed

to smell the gunpowder, to hear the hysterical audiences screaming for more! I remembered a guy with a long ponytail, bearing
the unmistakable signs of drug ingestion, still beating his hand
on the front edge of the stage long after the music stopped. There
had only been his imaginary tempo to sustain his energy. Up on
the stage, I could picture the Texans with the sledgehammer rock
and roll style wrapped in Father Time beards, who once turned
down a razor company's offer of a million dollar fee if they would
just shave their Spanish-moss growths and pitch a product.

I had to admit to myself, nostalgia was hitting me hard.

Earlier that evening, as I had prepared for my return to the
world of rock and roll, I had carefully eyed my wardrobe. The
occasion demanded just the right ensemble . . . now who was I
kidding? Sartorial statements were a trivial matter at this stage in
my life, I argued, and deserved a cursory thought at best. Yeah,
right! Three hours before the time to leave for the show I found
myself trying on and modeling no fewer than six different outfits
before I could make up my mind.

Get a grip, man! It's just a rock and roll show! I finally
snapped, and after taking more time and consideration than a
shuttle launch, chose attire based primarily upon function rather
than fashion, made of the most lightweight material I owned
which would allow me to sweat my ass off in relative comfort and
anonymity.

Finally, there I was at the Summit, arriving by what route I
had no idea. I couldn't recall a single detail of the trip. And there
was the sparsely occupied parking lot that soon would be packed.
I got out of my car, and noticed as I slammed and locked the door
that my seat was marked by the outline of my rear end, a silhou-
ette formed by sweat, although the A/C had been running fine all
the way into town. I was still sweating like hell, for that matter.
Weak grip, I grumbled to myself.

It was then time for me to make the long, long walk—maybe
all of a hundred feet—to the back door of the Summit. My plan
at this point was to throw myself on the mercy of the security

guard, and finally confront my fears of rejection. The last mile to the electric chair was a "Cotton-Eyed Joe" compared to this.

I looked around and started to walk.

Earlier I had envisioned being turned away, embarrassing myself in front of whatever throng of guests and VIPs happened to be on hand for legitimate entry, of futilely arguing that "I really did work for them for fifteen years. Honest!" That was the real reason why I was here so early, I had to admit. If I had to fade away into the humid Houston night, the fewer people on hand to see my humiliation, the better.

There was no crowd at all. Since it was three hours before the concert, I guess that was no big surprise. As I padded my way down the incline, the only person I could see was the security guard. He looked up from his newspaper and asked, "Kin I he'p you?"

Was his tone of voice gruff and unfriendly, or was it just me? "No thanks," I said. "I'm just waiting for somebody." I found that I couldn't ask the guy for anything. I was going to have to wait until I saw someone I'd known back in the old days.

The rent-a-cop returned his attention to the funny papers and I ostentatiously glanced at my wristwatch, as if I was being inconvenienced and was impatient for the arrival of some late friend. The guard took no notice. So long as I didn't pass the line that separated "in" from "out," he couldn't have cared less what I did. I was nothing at all to him.

On the outside, looking in . . . For the first time in my life I was at a ZZ Top concert without having the run of the place. I nervously paced back and forth, humiliation close to the surface even though not another soul was in sight. I felt like a mongrel dog begging for scraps at the backdoor of a greasy-spoon cafe.

But now, what was this? Here came someone out the door past which, unescorted, I could not go. I didn't recognize the young man, but he was obviously a crew member. He had one of the much-coveted laminated tour passes around his neck. Trying to sound casual, but with the authority of greater age, I asked him which band he worked for. After all, the legendary English bluesman John Mayall was the opening act for ZZ this time, and the kid might be one of his people. I didn't want to spill my guts to some limey roadie.

"I work for ZZ Top," the kid answered.

All right! Now I could throw a few names around to prove that I was cool and knew what I was talking about. It was a small relief, but I wasn't out of the woods yet.

"Are M.L., J.W., Donnie, Jimmie, or Bougre inside?" I asked.

The kid paused. He was looking me over curiously, no doubt wondering how this civilian knew the names of ZZ Top's senior crewmen.

"Sure, man. They're all inside eating supper."

Bingo! I had scored. Trying to balance out my shift from casual/authoritative to humble/demanding, an equally oxymoronic task, I said: "You can get this to one of them, can't you? I'd appreciate it."

I handed him a business card, the designation of my post-rock existence. I had ruled out bringing down my old stage pass from the ancient *Eliminator* tour as pure foolishness. No youngster would give a damn about an old has-been like me. It was either get a personal invitation from somebody or take a hike.

The kid took the card, squinted blankly at the meaningless name, and politely said that he would take it in to one of my name drops. He vanished back inside the huge building with card in hand. The guard, momentarily interested by the encounter, turned once again to the intellectual delights of "B.C." and "Peanuts." And I waited, watching the cars begin to fill the parking lot.

The next few minutes passed at the speed with which the Ross Ice Shelf moves toward the sea. As best I could I maintained the pose of being aloof and confident, pacing back and forth on the cement. I found myself actually whistling tunelessly and angrily cut it out. Whistling! It was a dead giveaway of how I felt.

The door opened. I looked up, and there walking toward me

175

I saw familiar old faces. Like mine, they were changed but still the same as before, the changes mainly being deeper lines and a higher forehead. The most rewarding part about this moment was that all of them were smiling. The road crew that had once been under my charge came out to greet me in groups of two and three.

"Hey, man. Long time."

"What's happening, dude?"

I hugged each one of them and shook their hands. We immediately began to swap old war stories, just as if the years hadn't drifted away into the past. They wondered, too, what I was up to these days. Seeing how that sort of banality would bore them quickly, I turned the conversation casually away, back to what really interested them, and me. The music, the Boys, the life of rock and roll.

It only lasted a few minutes before one of them glanced at his watch.

"Say, man. We've got to get back to work. Want to come on in and see the show?" Why else would I have been there at the backdoor of the Summit?

Someone came up with some comp tickets, in case a guard asked anything. It was a slight breach of courtesy to give comp tickets to an old road dog like me instead of a full-fledged backstage pass, but that was okay. I was disappointed, but I was in; they had probably long since run out of those babies. It was usually the case just hours before a concert. Larry "Fruitfly" Sizemore, the lighting engineer I had worked with on my last tour, these days had taken my old place and was ZZ's lighting director. He invited me to sit at the lighting console during the performance—a second unrecognized slight, but one that wasn't Larry's fault. He was extending as much of an invitation as he had control over. I would have to be satisfied with sitting out front instead of being backstage. And I would have to enter the Summit like the fans, through the front. As the guys headed back through the magic door, I headed for the entrance.

A short time later I walked inside, down to the floor level, and took up my station next to Fruitfly and his console. From there I could view the third of four sold-out shows in ZZ Top's hometown. We shot some bull as Fruitfly tinkered with his final adjustments, and I watched the seats start to fill.

Then the show started. John Mayall must have been good. He always is. I didn't notice, I was so pumped up. I only started coming back to reality when the lights came up for the set change, after Mayall had departed. All I was interested in was what ZZ Top was going to be doing that night. That was why I had come.

Now the house lights went down for the second time. The audience screamed and roared with anticipation as an intro tape of a woman reaching a very evident and satisfactory orgasm was fed through the massive ShowCo sound system. An orgasm at fifty thousand watts? It definitely got your attention. The shrieks and howls mounted, as one might say, to a climax.

All of a sudden the curtain whipped away to reveal ZZ Top's set: a junkyard complete with working crane, metal crusher, wrecked autos, and stacks of old televisions. There was Frank at his drum set, and on either side were "the Smith Brothers" of rock and roll. Billy's and Dusty's near waist-length beards flowed down from below their night-black shades. Once, a long time ago, I had nicknamed Billy "the Howard Hughes of Blues"; later I'd called him and Dusty "the Hughes Brothers." They had gotten maximum mileage and publicity out of a "look" unique to the twentieth century, and maybe to any other time as well. Maybe unique to any other planet bearing intelligent life. The Summit filled with a tumultuous roar of greeting which the Boys seemed not to notice or acknowledge.

That lasted for only a few seconds. Over the sounds of the crowd, the three Boys blasted into their first song. The massive building was enveloped by the driving beat of "Planet of Women." The cheering rarely stopped, continuing as a backdrop to the sounds being produced on stage. The power trio was doing its thing, strong as ever, and the crowd was eating it up just as in days of yore.

I knew the new tunes already. Some I had heard on the radio, some elsewhere; they were all on the newly issued album. The music was basically the solid Texas boogie as of old, raunchy Texas blues-rock delivered at full-tilt volume. It was new, yet the same, the sign that a firmly entrenched form of music had come to stay. And it was as good as it could be, meaning (in the milieu of rock) that it was "bad."

The three Boys played on, and I peered closely at them. They looked older, a bit timeworn; but you might say exactly the same thing about me. Time heals all wounds, and wounds all heal? Not exactly. It just flows on, and we have to flow along with it, like it or not. In this case, however, ZZ Top had slowed the process down some, and they were having fun doing it. You could tell by the enthusiasm of the set.

For me, it was fun watching the different special effects and lighting, the sort of things the fans never question and usually take for granted. Some of the cues and effects even looked a little familiar. Later Fruitfly would confirm that these were indeed ones I had created, which had been left in the show. The fans might not know it, but there was a little bit of me fixed into the firmament of ZZ Top. It was a supreme compliment, albeit an anonymous one.

The high point of the performance came when effigies of Billy and Dusty were lifted into a giant crusher and smashed. During this "crushing time" six well-stacked fems, donning cutoffs amounting to the equivalent of Levi butt-floss, cleared the stage of debris. The Demolition Debbies, as these lovelies were called, finished cleaning up the mess in a few minutes, in time to jiggle out of the way as Billy and Dusty motored back onto the stage encased in individual, remote-controlled mock-ups of compressed metal blocks, only their heads protruding from the top showing who they were. They roamed around the stage, acknowledging the cheers, then popped out of the contraptions sporting new suits for their finishing numbers and obligatory encores.

After the show ended and the lights came up, I stood around looking at the set. It was impressive. It looked like more money had been spent for this production than I had ever had to work with. The money machine that Bill Ham built out of ZZ Top and its music was clearly in working order, and I felt a touch of envy at how the power it generated could be used for enhancement of a show. Professionals tend to analyze things like that. I speculated idly on how I might have designed the set if I had still been involved.

Most of the audience was gone now. Different members of the crew came out front and talked for a few minutes. I said my good-byes, but glanced up at the stage now and then, wondering if I would be invited to speak with the Boys. By this time they knew I was here. If any of them wanted to see me, they would send a message.

I guess not. The minutes passed, the last of the crowd was gone. It was time to go.

I was just turning to leave when I saw three men in suits and cowboy hats walking toward me. I recognized one of them as ZZ's security chief Jim Lander, and I thought to myself, "Hot damn! They're sending ol' McCloud to come and take me back for a visit."

Well, not exactly. For Lander, despite my brief hug, this was not a teary-eyed reunion. He and the rest of the "country boy cadre" had been dispatched by Bill Ham to fetch me. "Bill wants to see you," he said. I thought about the dread those words held back in the old days, and realized it was still so.

Did I want to see Bill Ham? Probably not, I decided. If I went backstage I'd likely wind up listening to a diatribe about how I had deserted his happy musical family exactly when it needed me the most. I hedged, saying that I didn't have a pass, so. . . . But he interrupted me, whipping out a fistful of backstage passes. So that's where they all were! He handed one to me, then walked back to the dressing room area.

So what do I do now? I hemmed and hawed a little more with the farewells to friends, putting off a final decision. Then I was alone and had to make up my mind. What the heck. It wasn't like Ham could fire me a fifth time! I was already off the team. So I sauntered casually after Lander.

He met me at the access door of the hallway leading to the dressing rooms and escorted me through. Five feet away, lounging against the wall, I saw Billy Gibbons engrossed in animated conversation with a former NFL tight end who I think was Jamie Williams, a.k.a. Spiderman. Billy was doing most of the talking, as ever, and from what I could hear he was spinning another one of his tall tales. Whether totally factual, partly embellished, borrowed, or just plain bullshit, any yarn spun by Gibbons was always good listening. I stood about four feet away without saying a word, waiting for him to acknowledge my presence.

Although he looked straight at me every so often while he was talking, he never said a word to me. I'd like to think it was myopia, or that my looks have changed radically from the old days. Bill Ham walked by at one point, and he also failed to say anything. Now there was a surprise! Bill Ham pass up a bitchout/sermon session? He must be getting old.

Billy reached the end of his story. Now surely he would turn and say something. But no. Instead he was immediately whisked back inside the dressing room. I hadn't had a chance to even say hello before he was gone.

The hallway was starting to have fewer passersby. After ten minutes it was obvious that I was not going to be invited into the inner sanctum. Regardless that I had been a fifteen-year employee, personal friend, and *family* member, the fact that I had quit had made me *persona non grata*. I quietly left the building, got in my car, and began the drive home.

The feeling that swept over me as I navigated my way through the light traffic of the bright Houston evening was the

Circa 1979
David Blayney
in "Roller-
baller" guise
dreamed up by
Billy. The
whole crew
dressed this
way—really!
*(David Blayney
Archives)*

Circa 1981
O Lord, it's hard to be humble. Billy and the back of one of his many
custom guitars. *(David Blayney Archives)*

Circa 1983
Billy on the
Eliminator tour.
*(David Blayney
Archives)*

Circa 1983
Billy, Frank, and
Dusty on the
Eliminator tour.
*(David Blayney
Archives)*

1983
The answer is blowing in the wind, along with their beards. Billy, Dusty, and Frank. *(David Blayney Archives)*

1983
Bust the Dust: "Gimme All Your Lovin' " video shoot. *(David Blayney Archives)*

1983
Gina Thomasina, Frank, Danielle, Billy, unknown, Dusty, and video director Tim Newman: the cast and crew of the ''Gimme All Your Lovin' '' video. *(David Blayney Archives)*

1983
Sharp-dressed men or mechanics? Frank, Dusty, and Billy.
(David Blayney Archives)

1983
Management and labor on a road food stop.
(David Blayney Archives)

1983
Don Stuart and Larry Sizemore with essential equipment for the
Eliminator tour. *(David Blayney Archives)*

1983
Bad Wheels. *(David Blayney Archives)*

1983
After the "first take" of the "Gimme All Your Lovin' " video. Dusty signals #1 with his famous index finger — "The Pleaser." *(David Blayney Archives)*

Memorabilia from the road.
(David Blayney Archives)

antithesis of what I'd felt a few hours before. To my surprise I was relieved, no longer anxious with a sense of loss. The ending I had experienced was catharctic, like learning that a lost relative had indeed departed from this life.

It would have been nice, however, if one of them had just said a word or two to bridge the canyon from then to now. That would have been the right way to end things, to me. But they hadn't, so there you have it. End of story.

Each of us is just a human being, walking alone down the rocky path from birth to death. Human beings sometimes can get to be famous if they have talent, have a fair wind behind them, and somewhere along the way pick up a generous helping of luck. I realized that the Boys, with their strengths and weaknesses, honesty and bullshit, were no different from me. We had been young together, living a crazy life in a crazy time. Today we are getting on with our lives as best we can, each in his own direction.

You can never go home again, somebody once said. But as I have discovered, it's important not to let that fact bother you, because it *is* a law of nature.

MAKIN' TRACKS

The central purpose and primary fulfillment in life for a real musician is to make music.

A statement like that probably doesn't sound like much of a revelation, but there's more to it than you think. This is because there are more than a few people out there in this world disguised as musicians whose central purpose and fulfillment in life comes from making *money*. To them, music is a means to an end, not the other way around. These masquerading capitalists wielding instruments fall into the class identified as "entertainers." They surround themselves with enough quality musical support and/or electronic enhancements to disguise the fact that *they* are virtually without true musical talent.

And then there are true musicians who live to play and produce real music.

There are a fair number of Billy Gibbonses out there who may be just as good as he is, but who play for friends and on weekend gigs for little more than a few free beers. But if Billy's fate had been to be one of them, I don't think he would have had either a happier or unhappier life than it turned out. The same thing goes for Dusty and Frank. This is because they are *musicians* first and always. Money's nice, but without it . . . ? There would still be the *music*.

However, whether you are a real or a bogus musician, sooner or later you hope to wind up in a recording studio to cut some tracks, have some fits, carve some wax, maybe make some hits. The dif-ference between the musician and the entertainer is that the musician wants to put forth his best musical effort at *making* a recording. The entertainer's principal aim is to do well at *selling* the recording, regardless of quality, sincerity, or expertise. It's all a matter of emphasis.

Bill Ham had been a record promoter for H. W. Daily's record distributorship in Houston when the whole ZZ Top adventure got started. Because he was young, broke, and fairly inexperienced as yet at managing, Ham went into a fifty-fifty "gentleman's agree-ment" with the Daily family. There was no written document; neither side figured they needed one, since in the South your handshake is still supposed to be as good as your word. Ham would handle management of ZZ Top; the Dailys would handle finance. Bud and Don Daily have told me that they helped bank-roll the band up through 1973. That included buying band equip-ment and paying for some of the studio time for the first two ZZ Top albums. The Daily influence and assistance even went into helping to negotiate the original ZZ Top contract with London Records.

But the passage of time can change relationships, especially ones riding on a grip of the hands. Memories of specifics fade, conditions alter; everything gets tenuous. As ZZ Top started to generate a healthier cash flow, Bill Ham started whittling away at the Daily's percentage of the profits. It would be uncharitable to suggest that in Ham's view once the Daily's financial backing was

no longer needed, the relationship with them warranted altera-
tions. I won't say it, but you can infer anything you want to about
this. Thoughts come cheaper than rhetoric.

On two occasions Ham met with the Dailys to rearrange the
pie slice sizes, and they agreed to the changes. Then in early 1974,
after *Tres Hombres* was solidly up there in profits, Ham called a
third meeting to discuss slices yet again. The Daily brothers arrived at the meeting not too happily and without further ado demanded point blank, just exactly what did Ham think their percentage ought to be *now*?

Ham looked the Dailys in the eye and said, "Zero!"

That was not quite that. The Dailys brought legal proceed-
ings against Ham, hoping to retrieve something from their in-
vestment. In May 1974 *Tres Hombres* was certified gold, assuring
that the band would henceforth be a major musical contender. In
January 1975 the Dailys and Ham dissolved their partnership, assuring that the Dailys would henceforth not realize a cent from
ZZ Top. There was a complicated settlement out of court, involv-
ing cash and royalty arrangements with London Records. Even if
the total value of the settlement was as much as the rumored
$100,000, it amounted to pretty anemic compensation for the
Dailys.

ZZ Top's first three albums were recorded in Tyler, Texas, at a
place called Brian's Studios. This facility was nothing more than
a cinder block addition to a house located in a quiet residential
neighborhood, and looked more like a McCarthy-era bomb shelter
than a rock and roll recording studio. It was run by a zany character named Robin Hood Brian and his ever-present mother,
"Mrs. B." Robin's main claim to fame in Texas was his reputation
as the "jingle king." Many a catchy tune extolling the merits of
hamburger joints and hardware stores had been recorded in the
bomb shelter, and many more would be, long after ZZ Top scram-

bled up to more conventional recording environments. Robin's place was also known for being the home turf of that world-famous Texas band, *Mouse and the Traps*. It always used to make me tremble just a tad to think that I was once in the same studio as a legendary group like that.

Robin received ZZ Top's business for one very good reason: He was dirt cheap. Ham had gotten to know Robin through the record promotion business, and since they were friendly acquaintences, he probably got an even better deal on the ZZ Top recording sessions than Robin would have given anybody else. Having recording sessions up in Tyler, which is about a four-hour drive back into the Piney Woods of east Texas, also undoubtedly appealed to Bill Ham's fixation on keeping all his doings as secret as possible.

Extensive rehearsals of the band were always carried out long before a studio visit was organized, because even the little bit that Robin charged was mighty taxing to the Ham managerial budget until after the great success of *Tres Hombres*. Both *ZZ Top's First Album* and *Rio Grande Mud* were rehearsed back in the garage at Billy's parents' place. Despite the band's efforts to keep the noise down, they were, after all, an electrified boogie band; small practice amps and wall padding just weren't enough to permit the Gibbonses (or anybody on the block) to get much sleep when rehearsals were going on. So for *Tres Hombres* Billy and Ham lined up a vacant former post office building as a rehearsal hall. This place had the advantage of greater space, but while it was being rented, somebody had to stay on the premises all the time to make certain none of the equipment was "borrowed" by local riffraff. This meant that Pete and I had to camp out at the post office building, taking alternate evenings for the baby-sitting. Ham's security concerns seemed excessive; the place had been a post office, for Chrissakes! But on a slim budget, sweat equity forms your capital of choice, and we couldn't afford to lose a single instrument or amp.

The first few trips up to Robin Hood Brian's were exciting

and charged with energy. Bill Ham would drive the Boys in his car; Pete and I would follow in the truck with the gear, trying like hell to keep up. Ham always talked ninety miles an hour and drove a hundred. Whenever he had the Boys in the car with him, he liked to drive one-handed while sitting turned a quarter of the way around so that he could look at whoever was in the back seat. This mode wasn't conducive to particularly high marks in driver courtesy and safety; following along behind, Pete and I would watch in horror as Ham narrowly missed head-on collision after head-on collision. Those drives to Tyler with Ham probably brought the Boys closer to death than booze, drugs, or outdoor shows in the rain ever did, but he never realized it.

As they sped along the highways Ham would tell the Boys army stories or sing marching cadence or talk about "the bidness." On occasion they would even write songs. According to Dusty and Frank, *La Grange* was written en route to Robin's studio one time. Based on the speeds Ham drove, I can see why it turned out to be road-drivin' music.

Stopping along the way at funky barbeque stands, lunch counters, rural grocery stores, and whatnot was also standard practice. Billy referred to this as field research. He liked to study and then imitate the different Southern Black dialects he came into contact with. He exposed himself to as much Texana as possible for future use during the years leading up to the ZZ Top World-Wide Texas Tour.

I remember all of us stopping once by a pumping oil well. Billy got out of the car, climbed over a fence, and got up on the rig while it was moving up and down. He literally *rode* the thing. All the onlookers except one agreed that this was great sport, the one being Bill Ham, who protested ineffectually the whole time. Ham was nervous as a first-day nursery school teacher doing safety patrol at a street crossing, no doubt because if Billy fell or even just had one little finger pinched off, that was all she wrote with ZZ Top. Billy had that sort of wild streak in him, playful and foolish. Except when it scared him, Ham actually liked Billy's way of rushing helter-skelter through life, and would pretty much let him do whatever he felt like.

On another day we stopped by the side of the road to drain the dew off our lilies. I remember looking up after finishing my business, and there was Billy Gibbons pelting along on the white stripe in the middle of the highway, wearing nothing but a baseball cap, some black hightop tennis shoes, and an ear-to-ear grin. As Billy ran, his dong swung from side to side with each stride in metronomic perfection. Ham literally cried with laughter at the sight. Billy was a looney guy, all right.

When ZZ Top finally arrived at the studio, things were expected to proceed like clockwork. The gear would be set up, microphones put in place, sound levels checked, and away the Boys would go into recording mode. "Time is money, boy," Ham said repeatedly to anybody around.

This was when the hours spent rehearsing either in the cramped garage or the post office proved their worth. Since they had prepared so completely outside the studio, recording time for the basic tracks was minimal. Unlike some bands, ZZ rarely took time to write in the studio because it was expensive.

Billy spent the most time in the studio. This was natural, since he had to do more than one guitar part and most of the vocals. The basic tracks (rhythm guitar, bass, and drums) for each song would be laid down immediately. After those were completed, Dusty and Frank were essentially finished for the moment except for minor touch-ups and whatever vocals Dusty was to do. While they and we two roadies wandered around the yard or talked with Mrs. B, Billy and Ham would be in there with Robin honing the takes. A boogie guitar lead can be rehearsed up to a point, but after that you just sort of wing it. You may get that certain tone, riff, or nuance of play on the first take; sometimes you give up after thirty-five tries and take the best of what you tape. Despite the cost, Ham was always pushing Billy to give it one more try, to push for perfection. It was the perpetual benefit/cost squeeze.

Usually Billy was still game after laying down tracks all day, even when he had become exhausted and there was no way he could play his leads anywhere near perfect. Billy was usually calm and even-tempered, and after getting into meditation he became positively mellow. He was a producer's dream lead guitarist—highly competent and willing to work long hours.

Once, however, during the umpteenth try of a lead part for the first album, he showed some temper. He dropped a lick and ruined the take just when they thought it was going to turn out dead-solid perfect. Ham, seeing dollar signs with wings on them flying off into the sunset, called to Billy from the control booth, the most aptly named thing in the studio.

"Come on, Billy," he said. "Play the part right, son!"

Billy snapped back, "Why don't you come on in here and play it yourself?" This was followed by a pause so long and pregnant its water almost broke. Tension filled the air like gathering thunderclouds.

Ham finally mustered what amounted to a contrived half-chuckle. He said tamely, "Come on, son. Let's just make us a record."

Billy cooled off and went on to complete the take. It was one of the few times I ever saw him act macho offstage, a Mel Gibson yanking off the disguise of a Dustin Hoffman. It was very uncharacteristic of him and took everybody by surprise—especially Bill Ham. It seemed to change Ham's view of and approach toward Billy Gibbons ever afterward. You just can't force notes out of a musician like the last bit of toothpaste in a near-empty tube. Music has to flow at its own pace.

After this episode, and perhaps influenced by it, Billy changed his method of recording. He would still cut the basic tracks in the main studio room or in an isolation booth, with Frank playing in his drum cubicle and Dusty thumping away in his bass cubicle, each listening to the others through individual headsets. However, when it came to laying down his leads and other guitar parts, Billy decided to move himself and his amp into the control booth. This is a fairly standard practice in the industry today, but back then it wasn't so common. By doing this he could listen to his new guitar parts and the basic tracks simultaneously through the more powerful control booth speakers. That way he was able to adjust his amplifier more precisely, and get a more accurate assessment of how the new guitar parts blended with what was already laid down. Big speakers produced a fuller and more cohesive sound than the tiny headset speakers, plus it had to be more comfortable playing without those things on your head.

This control booth system sat Billy right next to Robin and Ham, so communication between them all became more direct and personal. It was much better than being a musical fetus at the distant end of an umbilical headset cable. While Billy was cutting a track, Ham sometimes would cheer him on. Since the speaker producing the sounds that were actually recorded was on the other side of a noise-proof wall, Ham could yell his ass off in the control booth when he thought he was "gittin' a good 'un" and not screw up what went on tape.

Ham could also suggest guitar variations by humming them for Billy between takes. During one of the *Rio Grande Mud* sessions I was sitting quietly with them and watched Ham hum part of the lead of "Francine" to Billy. Ham would hum it, Billy would play it. A regular rock and roll Rogers and Hammerstein, I laughed to myself.

But as it turned out, that was a rare moment for me. Eventually Ham restricted access to the control booth and basically allowed nobody else in there besides Billy and Robin. This came about after Pete and I offered some musical suggestions after hearing a playback one day. Shortly afterwards we found ourselves promptly and permanently evicted. We were essentially locked out ever afterward unless bringing in food or drinks. Even Frank and Dusty sometimes needed a control booth visa to find out what was going on. One sound engineer and one producer were enough! When I look back on it, I realize how right he was in doing this.

These recording sessions early in the 1970s were mainly a Gibbons-Ham love affair. It was the old "management-labor" split I mentioned earlier, and gradually became the source of some resentment. Billy and Ham controlled all aspects of the process, and Frank and Dusty were seldom called on for either opinions or advice. They simply cut their basic tracks and headed for the house until it came time to do vocals, add percussion parts, or do touch-ups. Most of the time the vocals were done last, and since Frank ain't no crooner, only Billy, Dusty, and Ham would go to the studio. The rest of us would just hang out in Houston until it was all done.

As the originator and leader of the band, Billy did pretty much whatever he wanted on the recordings with Ham's easy support in most matters. If Billy didn't like the way a bass part sounded, for example, on some occasions he would simply recut the part himself in secret. Pete once told me that he encountered Billy late one evening at the end of a recording session coming out of the control booth with a tangled mess of recording tapes in his hands and a satisfied grin on his face.

"What's all that?" Pete asked him.

"It's Dusty!" Billy replied, and then cackled as he tossed the exorcized bass part into the trash can. If Dusty ever knew about these goings-on, he chose not to mention it.

If you weren't actually in the studio watching the songs being stitched together, these visits to Robin Hood Brian's place got to be more boring than a P.T.A. spaghetti supper. The lustre of "goin' to record some hits" faded fast after Pete and I were banished from the control booth and reduced to the lowly status of errand boys. Our main function—for hours—was to fetch things, mainly basic provisions and cigarettes. Dusty periodically needed Kool cigarettes and something to drink; Frank was happy with Kools, orange juice, and massive quantities of Sweet Tarts. Billy's staple was barbeque sandwiches.

When we ostracized peasants weren't driving around Tyler looking for smokes and eats we were free to pursue scintillating conversational encounters with Robin Hood's mother. Mrs. B had a presence that would make Roseanne Barr seem like Mother Teresa. She was superficially cordial enough, but you could never get too comfortable around her. It was like trying to hang out with your school principal. She had no qualms about voicing her opinions about society, religion, or *you*, and did so frequently.

On one late, tedious night at Robin's, out of grinding boredom, Pete and I were watching the television news with Mrs. B. in her living room. The big story on the tube was about some black militants who had barricaded themselves the day before in a Howard Johnson's over in New Orleans, making some sort of statement that involved trying to burn the place down and having a major shootout with the local gendarmes. We perked up our ears because we had been in New Orleans the day before and actually had planned to stay in that very same motel, only winding up somewhere else through a freak chance. Pete and I even went over for a firsthand look at the action, retreating hastily when a major fusillade broke out from where the militants were making a last stand.

As the reporter went through the statistics of how many wounded and dead had been produced by the siege's employment of over 100,000 rounds of ammunition, the screen focused in on the final assault made by the New Orleans police. Several brave, albeit foolhardy tactical specialists were charging across a roof at full tilt, firing at the metal door behind which the remaining militants were presumed to be holding out. A ricocheting bullet wounded one of the cops. It was "Rambo *vs.* the Brothers," and I laughed out loud; Pete agreed with me when I volunteered the opinion that it was about as obtuse a police action as we had ever witnessed.

"You little bastard!" Mrs. B. screamed at me. "How would you feel if it was YOU? Those are brave men there!"

Needless to say, I didn't make Mrs. B.'s Christmas card list

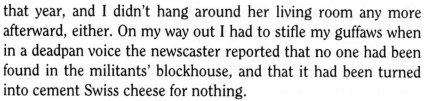
that year, and I didn't hang around her living room any more afterward, either. On my way out I had to stifle my guffaws when in a deadpan voice the newscaster reported that no one had been found in the militants' blockhouse, and that it had been turned into cement Swiss cheese for nothing.

A lot of criticism has been laid on ZZ Top's first two albums. The most common denigrating adjective used to describe the quality of the recordings is *unprofessional*, a highbrow way to say "more than slightly shitty." The drums sounded muffled, the guitars sounded muffled, the vocals sounded muffled, and in general the whole effect is as if all the tunes were recorded through cotton gauze. Strange as it may seem, the critics are wrong; this is exactly the sound that Billy and Ham wanted. They sweated bullets *creating* it; to them it made everything even more black and bluesy. Several albums later, when Robin and Mrs. B. were long-since history, I even overheard Ham suggesting that the band go back to Robin Hood Brian's place to ". . . get back that *fine* bluesy sound." Art is in the eye of the beholder, and music in the ear.

Part of ZZ Top's third album, *Tres Hombres*, was recorded at Robin's, the other part in Memphis at Ardent Studios. Ham developed a rapport with Ardent's owner after the split with the Dailys in early 1974—and with the improved cash flow that *Tres Hombres* produced, Ardent became the Boys' new recording home.

Talk about a step up! Compared with the studio in Tyler, Ardent Studios was the Taj Majal. There was vastly more room, better access for the band's gear, state-of-the-art recording equipment, candy and drink machines, a lounge with a television that could pick up more than two stations, and . . . no Mrs. B! ZZ Top's days of being strapped for cash were behind, and it showed in this place. With the pressure off, now the Boys could enjoy some of the finer things in life, and do some experimenting with their music.

This was also the point where Dusty and Frank obviously had a word or two with Billy and Ham about their status in the band. They wanted a full, even shake, and that was that. Billy and Ham pondered this situation. Maybe Dusty and Frank could have been replaced, but it would never be the same. A band's unique sound stems from the unique styles of each musician. Not only that, the band *mystique* that Ham was always so lathered up about depends to more than a small extent upon the factor of "cult worship" each band possesses. Fans come to adore a band's sound, and gradually each of the band members becomes an icon associated with it. Billy and Ham understood all of this, so they relented about equal status, and ZZ Top did not fall apart. Dusty and Frank got better treatment, namely equal album credits, and everything went along more smoothly.

As ZZ progressed to *Fandango*, then on to *Tejas, Deguello, El Loco*, and *Eliminator*, the use of new and different effects and instrumentation became necessary in order to keep abreast of contemporary high-tech musical trends. Billy, always a tinkerer, began getting interested in setting a few standards himself. The band continued to use the same approach of rehearsing all arrangements extensively before ever crossing the threshold at Ardent, but after the basic tracks were cut Billy began spending increasing amounts of time and effort trying to innovate for its own sake.

To give you an idea of what lengths he would go to, there's the story of "Billy and the Violin." One day Billy came into the studio with a violin under his arm to cut a background track for "Heartbreaker," written for the *Tejas* album. That in and of itself was nothing odd; we guessed that Billy had hired a fiddle player to knock out some notes for him, since he had never indicated that he knew too much about violin playing. But he quickly set things straight on that subject; he was going to do the dubbing himself! However, he encountered a mild setback right off; he didn't know how to *tune* a violin! So, since I was the guy who had tuned his guitars for him back in the old days, he handed the violin over to me and said, "Here, tune it."

What I knew about violins equalled what I knew about prostate surgery. Steve Deaver (alias Rod Reno), Billy's guitar tech at the time, was quietly standing right next to me taking this all in, and I seized the opportunity.

"Here," I said, giving the instrument to him. "*You* tune it."

Steve knew a lot about guitars, but this might have been the first time in his life that he had ever held a violin. Without a pause or a word he promptly handed the violin back to Billy, who now looked perplexed. If there had been any onlookers, they might have interpreted this little series of hot-potato Olympic relay exchanges as evidence that the violin was infested with crabs.

In the absence of any expert assistance, Billy finally managed to tune the violin himelf to some musical configuration. Since he knew a little bit about ukelele music, it may have wound up with some variant of the "my dog has fleas" tuning. Whatever it was, on the recording the finished product sounded decent enough.

Another time, when *El Loco* was being put together, Billy tried his hand—or foot—at playing pedal steel guitar for "Leila." Billy was highly competent on a variety of plucked string instruments, but as much as he tried he simply couldn't get the pedal steel part he wanted into any kind of shape. After many attempts and many failures, Billy finally gave up and called in custom guitar manufacturer and pedal steel player Mark Erlewine to play the part for him.

As far as I know, this is the only time Billy was ever totally defeated by an instrument. It was also very unusual that Erlewine's contribution was omitted from the album jacket and Billy got credit for the guitar part. This raised some eyebrows, since all musicians who work on a song generally have their names noted for posterity (and current reputation).

Billy never did get comfortable enough to play pedal steel guitar in concert. When ZZ Top went on tour, the guitar part and vocal to "Leila" were taken along on tape and experimented with for a few sound checks. Billy sat at the pedal steel guitar onstage and faked playing and singing as the tape ran. He asked me to try low-key lighting, hoping that the mimicry would be concealed. The end result looked good and sounded great (Erlewine is another wonderful musician), but after the sound checks Billy scratched all thoughts of doing the tune onstage. He just wasn't comfortable with that type of deception, and the tune was never used in front of a concert audience.

For *Deguello* Billy had gotten way into electronic enhancement and used about every guitar gadget he could find as the album was made up. He played through phase shifters, octave dividers, harmonizers, ring modulators, tone benders, digital delay, and any other gizmo or effect he could lay hands on. The result, naturally, was an amazing cornucopia of guitar sounds. When Jimmy Vaughn heard the album he called it "a treasure chest of tones." Billy greatly appreciated such praise from his old guitar shoot-out acquaintence, whose own career with the Fabulous Thunderbirds had made him a legend and critic whose voice was heard in the music industry, even if he was still "only sixteen years old!"

By the time *El Loco* came along Billy was a post doctoral student of synthesizers, vocal harmonizers, and numerous other gadgets, so the results on the album and (thanks to sound augmentation) onstage made ZZ Top sound more like an orchestra than a three-piece band. It is interesting to sit back and listen to one of the old *Rio Grande Mud* tunes, then switch over to anything off of *El Loco*. Yes, it sounds sort of like the same band. It also sounds like the band members hired some additional side men. But that's "show bidness." A band has to continually evolve musically to maintain the interest of the public. No change, no "change," you could say.

Probably the most dramatic development in ZZ Top recording approaches came about as *Eliminator* was constructed. What had gone on before was evolutionary; this change was revolutionary. ZZ Top got what amounted to a new bandsman (so to speak) for the album, unknown to the world at large and at first even to Dusty and Frank.

When you've got a fairly serious pile of gold to sit on top of, as Ham and all the Boys did after the turn of the 1980s, it's possible to indulge a fantasy or two. Frank had bought a large home on the southwest side of Houston, and after everybody got to talking once about how ZZ Top needed a private state-of-the-art rehearsal facility, he more or less volunteered to have one built in a wing of his place. It was a nice gesture; he wouldn't have to do any driving around town to rehearse, and he probably got a nice tax write-off to boot.

An old acquaintence of the Boys, Linden Hudson, was hired to build the studio. Starting with *El Loco*, the band began using Frank's place as their permanent rehearsal hall and test recording studio. Linden, as the electronic architect who had handled the studio's assembly, slid naturally into the role of permanent rehearsal engineer.

The facility's equipment was good, if not truly state-of-the-art; enough so that some of the synth and percussion parts recorded at Frank's turned up on the *El Loco* tune "Hippie Pad," somehow without Linden getting credit as the recording engineer. Linden never raised a stink about this, as he might have. This was partly because he went back with the Boys to 1970, when he was working as a radio disc jocky aliased *Jack Smack*. He was emcee for a show ZZ did around that time, and even sang an encore tune with the band, perhaps the only person ever to have that honor. The other reason Linden didn't complain about not getting his due credit for "Hippie Pad" was that Billy had a little talk with him on the subject of "rewards down the road." Shades of the promises to poor old Lanier Grieg over a decade earlier!

Linden remained at Frank's place as ZZ's live-in engineer throughout the whole period of *Eliminator* rehearsals, and was like one of the family. He figured that the *El Loco* sessions had

196

been a test more than anything else, and anticipated receiving credit when *Eliminator* was produced. For a virtually unknown producer/engineer, working with a major band like ZZ Top could be a big break. As he worked at the controls day after day, watching the album take shape, his hopes for a big step forward in his production career undoubtedly soared.

Eliminator marked the first time that ZZ Top was able to rehearse an entire album with all of the recording studio gadgetry Billy so loved. With Linden Hudson around all the time, it also was the first time the band could write, rehearse, and record with someone who knew the men and the machines. ZZ Top was free to go musically crazy, but also musically crazy like a fox. Linden made that possible, too.

Linden was a computer person, a technical dude, and a bit of a researcher. He got the notion of quantifying aspects of contemporary successful music to see what, if anything, they held in common. Getting into this involved the extensive examination of current hit song tempos. When he was finished, the research showed that the vast majority had one thing in common: They were all played within a beat plus or minus 124 beats to the minute. Linden inferred that 124 beats per minute must be the optimum dance meter for human beings. Excited, he suggested to Billy that if they used this formula in their music, ZZ Top could make a serious foray into the dance marketplace, an area their wind-up-and-go power playing had missed due to overdrive.

It was a startling idea. Billy studied the data for hours, fascinated. He ended with the decision to go after the hot rodders in the 124-beat mode. Maybe all the years of resistance to rock and roll by rednecks had a *physiological* foundation! If that was so, the *Eliminator* album would be yet another breakaway point for the band. They got down to the business of building the desired "magic meter" into the new collection of songs.

After his quantitative revelation, Linden informally but instantly became ZZ Top's rehearsal hall theoretician, producer, *and* engineer. Billy was the impetus behind most of the writing, since

Dusty and Frank weren't keen on practicing too much and Ham only dropped by every couple of weeks or so to see how things were progressing. Linden found himself in the position of being Billy's closest collaborator on *Eliminator*. In fact, he wound up spending more time on the album than anybody *except* Billy. While the two of them spent day after day in the studio, they were mostly alone with the equipment and the ideas. Frank was usually off playing golf; Dusty was just off playing around.

Nobody filled Bill Ham in on what was afoot; Billy was too excited about the music, and Dusty and Frank just didn't seem to think about it that much. Ham assumed that the music was being composed just as it always had been and left it at that. When at last Ham dropped by Frank's place to hear some of the music, he consequently didn't realize Linden's integral role in what had been going on. As the Boys and Ham were filing into the studio to get started, Ham's inclinations toward secrecy in all things got the best of him.

"Boy," he said to Linden, measuring the technician patronizingly, "We won't be needin' you now." Linden looked over at Billy, and Billy rolled his eyes. Everybody still deferred to Ham's wishes, so Linden got into his car and drove off to take in a double feature.

When he returned some five hours later, Linden found Billy sitting alone in the darkened studio, softly strumming his guitar without amplification. The image was spectral: a rock and roll star whose blues riffs on stage were so loud that they nearly blew out the lights was playing almost soundlessly in the shadows. Billy looked up with a friendly, quizzical grin.

"What's going on, man?" Linden asked curiously. Was it some new creative twist in Billy's mind?

Not hardly. The simple fact was that Linden was the only person around who knew how to turn everything on. Billy told him that as Linden was strolling out to his car unnoticed, the Boys were *trying* to explain to Bill Ham that Linden was the studio architect and integral to making the whole electronic concoction work properly. He had built it; moreover, it was his direct technical assistance that had produced what *Eliminator* was proving to be.

The manager's reaction to all of this was pure Bill Ham. "Ahhh, *I* can turn this stuff on!" And he began rooting around in the gear.

"I'm telling you, you shoulda been here," Billy laughed. "Ham was on his hands and knees for twenty minutes tryin' to find the right switches to turn on. When he finally realized that he couldn't do it, he left in a *bad* mood!"

Ham never again questioned having Linden at his station on the recording console. He probably didn't want to risk wearing out the knees of his best pants again looking for switches to flip.

The integral position Linden occupied in the process of building *Eliminator* was demonstrated eloquently in the case of the song "Under Pressure." Billy and Linden, the studio wizards, did the whole song all in one afternoon without either the bass player or drummer even knowing it had been written and recorded on a demo tape. Linden synthesized the bass and drums and helped write the lyrics; Billy did the guitars and vocals. Billy was so jazzed at the results that he immediately played the tape for Ham, without explaining the particulars of how the recording had been made. Ham agreed that "Under Pressure" was great music.

The next day, when Frank and Dusty were actually in the studio instead of out and about, Ham arrived just to hear "Under Pressure" played in the flesh by ZZ Top. When he asked them to play it, Frank and Dusty looked at Ham like two bulls at a bastard calf. What in the hell did he mean, play under pressure? ZZ Top *always* played under pressure! Neither of them had the faintest idea what Ham was talking about until Billy and Linden filled them in later. It was quite a while before Ham discovered that Frank and Dusty had not been around for the demo recording of "Under Pressure," if he ever learned the true situation.

That's the basic scenario. According to Linden, while Dusty

and Frank were exhibiting only peripheral interest in the development of *Eliminator*, he cowrote and arranged "Under Pressure," helped arrange chord and lead guitar parts for "Sharp Dressed Man," introduced the pumping synthesizer in "Legs," helped write the words to "I Got the Six," and injected some technical effects into "T.V. Dinners" and "Dirty Dog." Linden says that he was the guy who first screamed, "Hey! Get that dog outta my yard!" into the mic, which Ham insisted on having duplicated to the exact instant for the album version of that song.

There was also a song entitled "Thug" which was *entirely* Linden's baby, top to bottom, and unfortunately this was to become an issue that permanently ended Linden's association with ZZ Top. Linden wrote the song when nobody else was around. Billy heard Linden playing it when he arrived at Frank's one day and thought it was pretty hot. Not long afterward, as *Eliminator* was being recorded in Memphis, Billy phoned Linden to say that he had found somebody who was interested in the song, but nothing in the way of details was mentioned.

It was then that Linden realized he hadn't yet copyrighted "Thug." Copyrighting is always a wise idea in a business where borrowing is rife, and outright theft commonplace. In December 1982 Linden Hudson obtained his copyright for "Thug." With all the rehearsals over at Frank's place, he moved on to other things and forgot about the song.

That is, he forgot about it until he picked up a copy of *Eliminator* after it was released in April 1983 and discovered that "Thug" was one of the featured songs! Not only that but the name of Linden Hudson, the console magician who worked for weeks in the studio at Frank's place with Billy Gibbons as *Eliminator* was unfolded, appeared not one place on the album. The Boys had copyrighted "Thug" in April 1983, more than four months after Linden got there first.

The forthcoming line from Ham, as the Boys' representative, was that the song had been purchased outright from Linden. This argument was weakened by the fact that no bill of sale for the transaction could be located. After attempting to reason on the subject, it finally became obvious to Linden that his erstwhile friendship with the Boys wasn't going to get him anywhere. There wasn't much he could do about getting stiffed on the credits issue, but the records of the copyright were clear.

So, determined not to come up with a completely empty wallet, Linden moved out of Frank's house and sued. *Texas Monthly* magazine some while afterward reported that the matter was settled out of court for $600,000. Out of this sum Huey Meaux (who had published Linden's song) and Linden split two-thirds between them, the attorney's fee gobbling up the balance.

A $200,000 profit for one song sounds like Linden got a pretty good deal, but that was not the case. *Eliminator* went on to become a multi-platinum album, just as Linden had predicted when he and Billy were setting up the 124-beat tempos and arranging all the material. *Rolling Stone* eventually picked the album as number 39 out of the top 100 of the 80s. Linden Hudson in a fair world should have had his name all over *Eliminator* and gotten the just compensation he deserved. Instead he got ostracized.

Is anybody out there looking for a songwriter/producer/engineer with ghost credits for a platinum album behind him? If so, I know just the man to recommend to you. I find it hard to believe that the Boys intentionally set out to do a number on Linden, but sometimes you tend to forget where you came from. It's very easy to get both greedy and self-serving in "show bidness." But unless their personalities have changed radically from what I knew them as, the fault for what happened lies elsewhere.

Here are a last couple of anecdotes on the making of *Eliminator*. Both come from Linden Hudson, who may have a personal axe to grind, but they ring true, based on what I saw and heard myself.

Frank finished cutting his drum parts for *Eliminator* at Ardent, as usual long before the album's completion. He decided to return to Houston rather than kill time in the haunts of Memphis. Once the recordings were all straightened out, Billy flew back with copies of the finished product. Frank was naturally interested in hearing what everything sounded like, so when Billy dropped by it was understandable that he wanted to immediately crank up the equipment and give it a preview. For some reason Billy was hemming and hawing and wanted to talk a little bit first, but Frank insisted.

"Gimme All Your Lovin' " was the first tune on the tape, and when the initial drum beat sounded, Frank, with his fists clenched, shot up out of his seat like a missile out of a silo. "Who's that fuckin' drummer?" he shouted at Billy. Frank has a distinctive sound all his own, and the drum licks he was hearing definitely were *not* anything he had ever put on tape. Some studio black magic had gone on, it was clear.

Billy couldn't look at Frank, he was so discomfited, but in a small voice he explained what they had done in Memphis. A good portion of the drum parts that Frank had done for *Eliminator* had been "eliminated" without anyone telling him, or asking that he return to do them over. Instead, some of his drum parts had been redone by a Linn drum machine. Frank Beard, the mad drummer of ZZ Top, replaced by an *electric drummer*? Without his permission? What the hell was going on?

It looked like a fistfight might be coming up next, so Linden quietly left the two Boys to work out their problems in private. One was furious and the other was trying to offer more explanations than a preacher caught at a whorehouse. Whatever Billy came up with, knowing Frank, it wasn't good enough. Chopping a musician's parts out of an album like that is almost grounds for homicide, but Frank finally had to accept it. To start doing anything over at this point would be a calamity to the whole distribution process. In the end, Frank's drum contribution to *Eliminator* wound up being primarily the tom-tom overdubs which no one could argue against artistically.

After Frank got clean and sober in the late 1970s, he didn't practice drumming as much as he used to. He was spending his time outside, perfecting golf strokes instead of drum beats. It was almost as if when he off-loaded all the chemicals prior to doing *Deguello* his interest in drumming went along with them.

Frank's competence with the sticks had eroded; as with every other skill, you use it or you lose it. From all indications, Billy was fed up with what he seemed to feel was subpar drumming. Linden recalls driving around Houston with Billy one night playing the *El Loco* tape on the car stereo, and Billy complaining that Frank's playing sounded "sloppy." It was then that Linden inadvertently injected the idea of a digital drum machine into Billy's already gadget-prone mind, with the result being Frank having to share playing time with a machine.

Yes sir. Billy always used to tell Dusty and Frank, back in the old days, "Just lay down the bed and I'll play on top of it." The attraction of seeking out musical perfection through a non-argumentative, digitized drummer to lay down a perfect drum bed had been stronger than faithfulness to Frank, who probably would have practiced his heart out to keep his licks in there.

One other from Linden Hudson's memory banks: After Billy persuaded Ham to wheel in a machine to augment some of Frank's drum parts, it caused problems with Dusty's bass parts. He had gotten so used to Frank's slushy style of drumming that he simply couldn't adapt to the Linn drum machine's perfect meter as his rhythm counterpart. This was understandable, since Dusty had been playing with Frank for over fifteen years. They tried the machine at rehearsal once and even Dusty agreed that it didn't work. Consequently, a good portion of the bass parts on *Eliminator* are compliments of a trusty Moog synthesizer, adjusted to Billy's tastes. On "Thug" Dusty made no bass contribution whatsoever, because try as he might, he couldn't duplicate the bass picking and fretting techniques that worked with the song. As you may have guessed, Billy played the bass part. But he didn't take the credit.

Don't confuse this studio application of technology with the Milli Vanilli scandal. They used stand-in singers in the studio *and* used taped vocals live, while they merely lip-synced. Their whole process was a sham. The members of ZZ Top *can* and *do* deliver the goods live, as anyone who has seen them live can attest. You really can't fault their desire to try to capture perfection in the studio. Based on the success of the *Eliminator* album and tour, they must have done something right.

Eliminator did more than eliminate the competition and dropkick anybody else who got in the way. Billy Gibbons was finally able to achieve his ultimate dream: perfect lead on top of perfect bass and perfect drums. The gadget fetish had been pushed to the limit. He had rebuilt ZZ Top in the studio as a trio with two machines as side men! *Eliminator* probably has the unique distinction of being the first high tech album to go platinum in which artificial musicians outnumbered the real ones.

I wasn't around to see what hijinks went on when ZZ Top did *Afterburner* in 1985, but there's no reason to think that things were much different than in the case of *Eliminator*. Unless ZZ Top had *no* live contributors left by now, and the machines did it all. Maybe machines played *lead* guitar parts as well as bass and drums, and the vocals were done by Max Headroom. I don't know, but if possible *Afterburner* sounded even more techno to me than *Eliminator*. *Recycler*, on the other hand, while full of state-of-the-art effects, is a return somewhat to the pacing and styling of their earlier albums. It makes you wonder if ZZ Top realized that there might be a limit past which too much technology is overkill and begins to distort genuine feelings. Sometimes you need to step back a bit from it all and return to your roots.

But does it *really* matter how the music gets to you so long as it's delivered? Isn't *making* music the objective? When it's time to deliver it *live* you can't do zany choreography or change tempo dynamics with a machine. To pull off a live concert you need some kick-ass musicians with feelings and emotions like Billy Gibbons and Dusty Hill and Frank Beard, doing what they've always done best—giving a kick-ass show. But how long can it last?

Apparently RCA records thought the Boys had a little more left in them, because in 1992, after Warner Brothers and Bill Ham decided not to continue their relationship, ZZ Top signed a five-album deal that reportedly could amount to over 40 million dollars. Given their track record of releasing albums years apart, I guess we can look forward to seeing them boogie on into the twenty-first century.

Back in 1974, Bill Ham took out an advertisement in *Billboard* magazine. It read, simply: "The truth is, ZZ Top is the truth." I believe that statement was accurate at the time. ZZ Top played kick-ass Texas boogie capable of ionizing your average skyscraper or cauterizing the fungoid insides of your head. In a day of maximum use of chemicals, rock and roll was clean and unsynthesized, clear and unsynthetic. You saw and heard what you got, and what you got was more than you sometimes expected.

Then came the gadgets, which some feel is like manifest deception.

What is ZZ Top today? The answer lies in individual translations of their recordings and live performances, which speak for themselves like all other music, and *that's* the truth.

Or is it?

It's for you to decide.

APPENDIX I

BILLY GIBBONS

Billy is simultaneously the best known and least known of the ZZ Top circus. His lead guitar virtuosity, the fact that he is the last remaining charter member of ZZ Top, and his songwriting have earned him a high profile in the music business, as he deserves. At the personal level, however, he remains nearly opaque. What is the *real* Billy Gibbons all about? Ask him one day and you. get one answer; ask him the next day, and everything has changed. The words you get depend upon his mood of the moment.

Some "Billy watchers" think that his ad libbed approach to things indicates a uniquely original mind in perpetual motion. They're right. Everything else about him points in the same direction. He craves the unusual and different. When not on tour he is rarely at home. Instead he is off on a trip somewhere, travelling around seeking out oddities and lore which will be filed away for future use.

If by some accident you do catch him at home, you will be struck by the sparse furnishings, the antique drugstore display rack filled with unused, plastic-wrapped "cheap" sunglasses, and the jukebox in the living room offering a montage of selections in blues, country, Tex Mex, contemporary rock, and a sprinkling of unusual titles and artists on obscure labels. You may see some of his humorous illustrations, frequently sent to friends on postcards, completed or partly finished. Bill Ham had (and may still have) a collection of Billy's skilled cartoon spoofs of Dusty drawn on airplane cocktail napkins. But there is very little sign of permanent occupation; open a kitchen cupboard and about all you will find is sixty or seventy cans of Mexican hot sauce and a sack or two of tortilla chips.

ZZ Top's songs almost always get their start in Billy's mind. There is no telling when and where a new song will be born. Once he showed me a spiral notebook in which he had jotted down about four dozen titles to future songs. When the creative juices are flowing, things usually begin with Billy fooling around with a guitar riff. At some point the melody he wants is there. Oddly enough, the usual next step is to apply a title, drawn either from the notebook or inspired by something he sees or hears at about that time. Sometimes earlier, but usually about now, is when Dusty and Frank come into the picture to work out the arrangements and communally help with the lyrics.

If he has a choice between something humorous or something that would only make sense to a nuclear physicist, Billy will always select what is fun—or funny. His antic personality was already obvious in high school. After he started his rocking and rolling all the stops were pulled and none have ever been put back in. His jokes and pranks are endless, frequently shocking to the graying generations, and always hilarious. About all he takes seriously in life are Mexican food, barbeque, hot rods, guitars, and his music.

One of Billy's favorite show-stoppers is to peel his laundry at the drop of a hat. Usually this is for select friends and acquaintences, but every once in a while he violates the proprieties in public. At a small college show in Colorado around 1972, for example, the opening act was doing its thing when Billy popped out of his dressing room door behind the speaker stacks wearing nothing but a rubber snake. For several minutes, *almost* concealed from the audience and in full view of the backstage crew, Billy bumped and grinded like a Vegas-show-girl-cum-Bourbon-Street stripteaser. The naked ballerina/snake charmer choreography was over-the-edge funny.

Another striptease of Billy's, this time sans any snake except the one nature gave him, was caught on film in a dressing room in Jackson, Mississippi. Dan Mitchell, ZZ Top's original drummer, was with us as "guest roadie of the week" and had a little 8-mm movie camera he swung into gear as Billy pranced and danced. Dan still has the film and periodically shows it off to buddies. Perhaps some day it will wind up in a ZZ Top video.

As much as taking his clothes off is a kick in the ass for Billy, donning wacky stage costumes also gives him a comedic charge. He has played shows in hot pants, as I mentioned elsewhere in this book, but that amounts to only the tip of the iceberg. In honor of the most famous rodent in North America, he did an entire night on stage in a homemade androgynous Mickey/Minnie Mouse outfit consisting of black leotards, a black pleated skirt, a Mouseketeer cap, and a cloth-wrapped, bent clothes hanger for a tail. Hell, on St. Paddy's Day I've seen him wear a green plaid suit with red checkered boots, emulating a wigged-out Irish Pee Wee Herman. Imagine what all the years have been like for Dusty and Frank playing behind such a deranged clotheshorse.

On the later tours, Billy's love for bizarre fashion statements began to spill over onto the crew. For the *El Loco* tour he outfitted the entire entourage of twenty-plus crewmen—the ZZ roadies, lighting crew, sound crew, riggers, truck drivers, and bus drivers—in skin-tight black nylon jumpsuits, plus plastic bicycle helmets rigged with football face masks, arm pads, and knee pads. This "rollerball" look was so menacing that it had to be scrapped for the European segment of the tour. The suggestion of state secret police in the twenty-first century was just too much for countries where people well remembered Hitler's Gestapo. To solve the problem, Billy had us swap the head gear for matching, continental-style berets and ZZ Top sweatshirts.

The favorite target of Billy's garment dementia was his long-time guitar technician, Jimmy Emerson, who in essence became Billy's life-sized Ken doll. Billy put together a number of different costumes for Jimmy to wear during the shows. When he materialized from the shadows at the side of the stage to hand Billy a guitar, he might be Billy-garbed as an Arab sheik with headgear and flowing caftan; a genie from a lamp in turban, harem pants, and curly-toed shoes; a chef with stovepipe hat and white uniform; or the stereotypical mad medico complete with lab coat, fright wig, and stethoscope. Jimmy was a kaleidoscopic human cartoon, courtesy of Billy Gibbons.

Manic he is, but out of the ether can come a totally different Billy. He is the least flexible of the three band members when it comes to making compromises. If he decides that he wants something his way, that's it. It *will* be his way. And he can act moody at times. Sometimes Billy would come to a sound check the afternoon before a show and not say a word to anyone. He would silently strap on his guitar, give a cursory grunt into his mic to test his vocals through the stage monitors, and then play a couple of songs in total silence, letting Dusty sing instead. If you spoke to him, perhaps asking a question, he would either nod his head or walk away without answering. It was hard to fit these pieces into the puzzle of Billy Gibbons. Was he unhappy, or pissed at something or someone—or just playing one of his mind games? Only he could tell you, and he wouldn't.

Whatever his inner self may be, in the band-member category, Billy Gibbons is one of the best tour leaders around. Some band members choose to distance themselves from the crew. Billy likes to stay close to the crew. He is deeply interested and involved in all aspects of the production. He talks personally with everybody, thereby getting in-depth knowledge of what each person does and how he does it. And if he's not riding in the semis on short trips to get a feel for the problems of moving the show around, he's using his versatility in mimicry to provide many laughs for America's long haul truck drivers over the CB radio.

Just as humor is Billy's guiding philosophy of life, the understanding of music and its making is his definition. Consequently, his song lyrics and vocal style are usually humorous. He has been a board member of the Contemporary Arts Museum in Houston and he was a founder of the Delta Blues Museum in Clarksville, Mississippi, honoring one of his musical heros, the late Muddy Waters. He had a guitar made from a plank taken from the shack that was Muddy's birthplace (the "Muddywood") to add to an extensive private collection of electric guitars and amplifiers, several of which he has donated to various causes. He has designed many guitars, most with exotic shapes and names such as the "Skrotchtone," the "Chiquita," and the famous spinning "Ultra Bush" series seen in the "Legs" video. And true to his love of custom 'rods, Billy recently built a successor to his *Eliminator* car, a chopped '38 Cadillac named CadZZilla that has appeared in several national hot rod magazines.

At this writing Billy Gibbons is living the single life. He has never married and I'll bet he never will.

DUSTY HILL

Dress up Dusty and you can take him anywhere for a drink or an evening. Of course, he'll still look the same dressed up or not, but he'll go along with you. Dusty just always manages to carry the same look all the time, no matter whether in robes or rags. As a fashion barometer, Dusty is perpetually fair to partly cloudy. Next to his bass playing style, sartorial confusion is what some people remember most about him.

He just doesn't have the natural physiology to wear clothes. I'm sure his success has afforded him the luxury of tailored and trendy fashions by now, but in the early days dressin' the Dust for a stage show involved some choices. It wasn't intentional, but somehow he automatically eroded the integrity of any rig into an "old" look, even before his beard. We tried dozens of clothing assemblages for him with identical results.

Put Dusty in a safari outfit and he became the *old* hunter; put him in a pea jacket and captain's hat and he became the *old* salt; mess up his hair a little, strip him down to his briefs, and he became the *old* wrestler. Before the beard it was a never-ending struggle for Bill Ham to keep Dusty from becoming the *old* bass player, not the sort of stage mystique a young rock

211

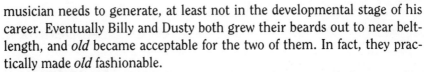

musician needs to generate, at least not in the developmental stage of his career. Eventually Billy and Dusty both grew their beards out to near belt-length, and *old* became acceptable for the two of them. In fact, they practically made *old* fashionable.

While Billy Gibbons may cook up some outfits seemingly from another universe, they always have parts that fit together. This has rarely been the case for Dusty. He looked his best in the early 1970s. The Boys tried British long-sleeved three-button T-shirts for their shows in the *First Album* days, which did the young and svelte Hill fine. After that Dusty tried a macho working-class hero look with boots, Levi's, and a denim shirt. No hat was needed because at this time Dusty still had most of his hair. He looked great and can be seen sporting this outfit in a picture on the inner sleeve of ZZ's *First Album*. He had short hair and and close-cropped beard and moustache, and looked young and virile. But macho working-class hero wasn't really Dusty's thing either, and a little time on the road ate up young and virile's ass. Dusty had to renew his search for a different and unique look. Different and unique he tried for; weird is what he got.

Dusty sashayed through an array of you-name-it hats, velvet luminescent pants, satin shirts, silk scarves, chain belts, leather pouches, snakeskin boots, and gaudy jewelry of all sorts. Whatever the costuming, it never seemed to come together in a single *unified* look. The Dust was a fashion banana split: Jimi Hendrix after a head-on with Jed Clampett; Bruce Springsteen's wardrobe mixed together with that of Michael Jackson. Billy got so fed up with some of Dusty's concoctions that he had Pete Tickle and me permanently "misplace" certain things so that Dusty couldn't wear them anymore. We had a big box down in the warehouse where we put all the stuff, which collected over the years and became quite a pile. After about a decade of accumulation, one day Dusty accidentally stumbled upon the cache. He was more excited and delighted than if he had found the Treasure of the Sierra Madre. I'm not certain he ever found out they had been intentionally hidden from him.

Early on in his career with ZZ Top Dusty began to exhibit male-pattern baldness, partly due to genetics but more likely attributable in a major way to all the blue dye jobs that scorched his scalp while he was with his former band, the American Blues. He eventually got into wearing hats because of this; Billy Gibbons did the same thing for the same reason. For a short period prior to hats, however, Dusty manifested an Oriental, or more specifically, a King of Siam/Daddy Warbucks look. One night before a gig, he had Pete and Frank shave his head. They left only a foot-long scalplock in the back, and then styled his moustache and beard à la Fu Manchu. The results seemed exemplary to Pete and Frank. There before them, looking out of occidental blue eyes, was a psychotic biker Cossack! Just the thing for the next show.

When I picked up Billy in my van that afternoon, after I had collected Dusty and Frank, he wasn't prepared for Dusty's latest adjustment of mystique. He did a cartoon double-take at his bass player when he saw him sitting back there in the lotus position. Billy's face took the expression of a drunk waking up with an ugly stranger. Have mercy! It's Taras Bulba as a Hell's Angel! For once, unintentionally, Dusty had gotten a lick back for all the Mickey Mouse, hot pants, and leprechaun costumes with which Billy had hit stage.

Dusty is also known for being the only member of the band to go down in the heat of battle. As a matter of fact, it was the heat of battle that made him go down, twice.

The first time was at an outdoor show in Virginia Beach, Virginia, circa 1972. The concert site was an abandoned landing strip and the time of year was midsummer. Out on the tarmac in the afternoon heat it was 100 degrees ambient and 110 degrees reflected. There wasn't a cloud in the sky or a tree to provide some vestige of shade for the crowd; moreover, the promoter was too cheap even to give the band shade on the stage. Right in the middle of "Goin' Down to Mexico," one of Dusty's few lead vocal songs, before 10,000 sweating fans, he suddenly keeled over face-forward, spread-eagled on his bass. Old Thumper was out cold. He had "gone down" during "Goin' Down."

With one-third of ZZ Top derailed, Billy and Frank looked at each other like they had just witnessed a drive-by shooting. Then with wide eyes they looked over at me. Still playing away, firing on two cylinders, they watched as I ran up and knelt over Dusty. I momentarily thought about pretending to give him last rites like a Catholic priest, but this was serious. I got him groggily onto his feet, then led him behind his speaker stacks for some cold water in the face and down the throat. In a few seconds he came around enough to wobble back out for the song's conclusion, but still not in good enough condition to sing the last verse. Billy sang it for him for the first and only time ever.

At another summer show in Fargo, North Dakota, the threat of rain had resulted in a scheduled outdoor show being uprooted and moved from a spacious racetrack into a cramped 10,000-seat corrugated tin barn that eventually doubled as a microwave oven. About 25,000 tickets had been sold and at least 15,000 of the ticket-holders managed to wedge into the building. All that body heat, plus the sun on the roof, plus the stage lights put

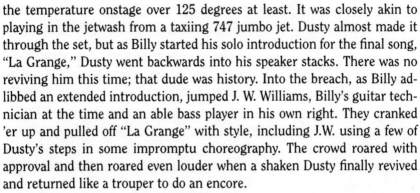

the temperature onstage over 125 degrees at least. It was closely akin to playing in the jetwash from a taxiing 747 jumbo jet. Dusty almost made it through the set, but as Billy started his solo introduction for the final song, "La Grange," Dusty went backwards into his speaker stacks. There was no reviving him this time; that dude was history. Into the breach, as Billy ad-libbed an extended introduction, jumped J. W. Williams, Billy's guitar technician at the time and an able bass player in his own right. They cranked 'er up and pulled off "La Grange" with style, including J.W. using a few of Dusty's steps in some impromptu choreography. The crowd roared with approval and then roared even louder when a shaken Dusty finally revived and returned like a trouper to do an encore.

The Dust played a little football in high school, but gave up a gridiron career after one year. This was because one day in a pileup somebody stepped on and thoroughly squashed the index finger of his right hand. When the wound healed, it left a rounded tip, sort of like a thermometer bulb, subsequently handy for bass playing . . . and other things. To this day he refers to this finger as The Pleaser.

Although somebody with his fair complexion and sensitivity to heat is an unlikely outdoorsman, Dusty is interested in guns and shooting. He occasionally tries his hand at trap and skeet, but handguns are more his favorite thing. The small collection of pistols he has accumulated over the years includes a Colt .45, which he likes to quick-draw empty. Occasionally he would have friends over and stage mock gunfights with "unloaded" weapons. I participated in a few of these, but I made damn sure I personally checked the gun Dusty used. You don't get old bein' a fool.

In 1984, several months prior to the *Afterburner* tour, he took a bullet in the gut amid mysterious circumstances. The story in the paper said that a Derringer in his possession fell out and discharged as a lady friend was helping him out of his boots. The version I heard was that the ersatz Annie Oakley was pissed off and simply popped a cap in him. Ouch! Better watch them "old hides" a little closer, Dust!

Of the three members of ZZ Top, Dusty always struck me as the one most prone to loneliness. He was always "on" in public, and is at home in the limelight, but off tour he spent a lot of time out of sight and by himself. For hours at a time he would just sit and watch the tube; that's how Frank came to tag him with the nickname Groover McToober, after the Zap Comics couch potato.

Sometimes Dusty would call me up at three in the morning, inviting me over to watch old Elvis movies with him. While we half-watched "El," a fair amount of the time, Dusty waxed philosophical about music in general. Bass playing is second to singing for Dusty. Ironically enough, he enjoys singing Gene Pitney-type ballads. Over the years he has written songs of this sort which could never be performed by ZZ Top. I wouldn't be surprised if he records some of his own tunes some day, if Ham's iron-handed clutch on Dusty's mystique relaxes some.

At this writing Dusty Hill is living in Houston. Sometimes he and Billy can be found cruising the posh clubs in a chauffeured black stretch VW limo. His name makes it into the society columns when he attends events frequented by the movers and shakers. His face has made it on TV a time or two during the N.B.A. playoffs. He and Tim Allen of the current hit TV show "Home Improvement" have become friends, and there was talk of ZZ appearing in a future episode. If that ever happens, I hope Dusty has enough sense to keep The Pleaser out of the line of fire of Tim's hammer.

His marriage yielded a daughter, Cody Jo, but unfortunately the marriage didn't last. At this writing he is single.

APPENDIX III

FRANK BEARD

Of the three members of ZZ Top, I was the closest to Frank Beard. We spent the most time together on and off the road, and we were roommates during the early 1970s. My experiences with Frank were highly varied, often raucous, and never dull. He was one of the most totally unpredictable characters I have ever known. This was due in part to chemically induced manic-depressive mood swings, but he was also just a wild and crazy guy out to have some fun. He was constantly getting himself into memorable situations.

I'll give you an example or two. I came home late one evening to find Frank crashed and burned on his bed wearing nothing but his body hair. There was nothing unusual in that, since Frank always slept in the nude. The thing that caught my attention this time was that at the foot of his bed, staring down at the *au naturel* drummer, were two teenaged girls! There was nothing kinky or illegal going on here; Frank was just sleeping peacefully while the young ladies, fully clothed, I might add, looked at him with the same innocent curiosity I'm sure they manifested in their home economics class at school, scrutinizing a soufflé. When I asked what was going on, they said that they had just brought him home and put him to bed. That was all.

He had needed it. Earlier he, I, and a guy we knew as Legendary Larry had rambled around town in Larry's Volkswagen and got backed up on some good "down brownie." In the midst of a visit to some friends, Frank excused himself so that he could nod out in the car, a common courtesy he often bestowed upon the fortunate. When Larry and I stumbled out some time later, Frank and the car were nowhere to be seen. Frank had awakened disoriented and had driven away in Larry's bug, leaving us stranded. Under different circumstances, that would have been called grand theft-auto. In this case it was just old Frank, one more time.

The girls told me they had noticed Frank driving slowly down the wrong side of a street, not a good idea for a hippie in a VW in Houston circa 1970. Getting Frank's attention over the high-pitched grinding sounds of the stretched-to-its-limits VW engine had taken some doing. After he faded in enough to understand what they were saying, Frank had asked if they would lead him to his address, and the amused girls agreed. They got him home, but as it turned out, without Larry's beetle. Since Frank had driven most of the way in second gear, he burned up the engine and wound up having to abandon the unfortunate VW by the roadside. He finished the trip home in the girls' car.

That was bad news for poor Larry, who had just recently had his motor tuned to perfection; worse news was that Frank didn't have the cash at that stage of ZZ's career to pay for a new engine. It took a while for him to compensate Legendary Larry for that episode.

On another occasion I came back to the house to find Frank laid up in bed (again) with a black eye and his lips swollen like a Ubangi tuba player. It turns out he had been playing a little pool in a local bar and had a disagreement with one of his fellow sportsmen. Frank lost the argument. That was another characteristic of Frank; sometimes his mouth would write checks that his ass couldn't cash.

Frank was nicknamed the Merry Frankster because of all the tricks he played on people. He would do things suddenly and unexpectedly, like walking up behind an unsuspecting roadie victim and yanking his trousers down around his knees—right in the middle of the stage during a sound check, while an accomplice captured the event on film. He did that one enough so that the ZZ Top roadies developed a behavioral pattern a psychiatrist might have interpreted as paranoid-defensive—constantly looking over their shoulders whenever Frank's exact location wasn't known for sure. Another favorite maneuver of his which added to the paranoia was to ease up behind a roadie engaged in conversation (preferably with a female), surreptitiously break wind, and then nonchalantly move away to let the innocent victim deal with the explanation. What a card.

Frank was and is the athlete of ZZ Top, as might be expected of a drummer. Billy ran a little track, and Dusty played a little football, but both have long since left any shred of an athletic past behind them, although playing a live performance four or five times a week while on tour would have to qualify as keeping in shape on a part-time basis. Frank has always loved to organize softball games and pit his team against another, usually for a wager of some kind.

While the two guitar-playing Boys fell into the general pattern of indoorsmen, Frank has kept energetically in shape and outside in the sun. He developed a passion for golf in the early eighties, to the extent of buying a house right on the fairway of a suburban country club. All he had to do was drive his customized golf cart out of its own private garage and head for the first tee.

But now his present passion is racing Porsche GT cars. True to his extremist nature, he has plunged neck-deep into this motor sport. He raced at Daytona in early 1993 and came in second in his class. This from a guy who was absolutely the worst driver I had ever ridden with. Frank mentioned in an interview that after he managed to get his car sideways in eleven out of the twelve turns on his training course, his driving instructor told him that he had "amazing recovery skills." I'm convinced that I was riding in a car with Frank at the wheel on many occassions when he was honing those "skills."

These days, if you can't find him on the links, or racing his cars, you might find Frank restoring and reselling 1960s vintage muscle cars.

Frank used to live a lot harder than he does today. Some of the signs of that period linger on, such as his interests in playing poker and shooting pool. The *big* change for Frank came in the late 1970s, when he managed to successfully kick the chemicals and get himself straight. He flirted with death, decided that he wanted to live, and did what it took to make that happen.

Frank is the only member of ZZ Top to be married at this writing, and in fact single-handedly has been married more than the other two-thirds of the band put together. His teenage marriage was doomed from the start, and probably so was the one during his drugged-out period. Today he is happily married to his third wife, Debbie, and they are the parents of twin sons, Nico and Rory. They are currently raising horses on a ranch in Fort Bend County near Houston on a spread named, appropriately, the Top Forty Ranch. Beating the odds, the former addict has become a solid family man.

IN BETWEEN THE GROOVES

Following is a song-by-song listing of ZZ Top's albums with comments as and if they came to mind.

Z.Z. TOP'S FIRST ALBUM (1970)

Confusion about ZZ Top's name stemmed from this album title. Years afterward people were still asking about "the Z.Z. Tops." Bill Ham also had to fight a war with the media and promoters for a few years with regard to the periods after the initials "ZZ." Any time he saw a marquee or an advertisement spelling the band's name with periods after the Z's, or two P's on *Top*, he would have the offender immediately correct the error.

"(Somebody Else Been) Shakin' Your Tree"
"Brown Sugar." Billy Gibbons tried to be soulful with a song about heroin.
   I don't think he ever did any, although Pete Tickle told me Billy once
   snorted some.
"Squank." ZZ Top sings about ecology.

"Goin' Down to Mexico." No true-blue Texas band could put out an album without a song about heading for Mexico.

"Old Man." This was the first of a series of songs in which Billy played guitar through an organ speaker called a Leslie.

"Neighbor, Neighbor." Pete Tickle wrote one of the guitar passages.

"Certified Blues"

"Bedroom Thang." Frank was totally exhausted after the final—of many—drum takes.

"Just Got Back from Baby's." This is one of Bill Ham's favorite ZZ Top blues songs.

"Backdoor Love Affair"

RIO GRANDE MUD (1972)

The album's front cover photo was not taken in the Rio Grande; more prosaically, it was taken in a bayou near Billy's house in Houston's Tanglewood subdivision, not too far from where ex-President George Bush built a house. The back cover photo was taken at the Coliseum in Houston, Texas, the day after Billy first saw Duane Allman play. It was the one of ZZ's best shows ever. Duane had obviously made a tremendous impression on Billy.

"Francine." Depending on whose story you believe, Billy either wrote this one with Steve Perron and Kenny Cordray or he horned in on the credits by custom-arranging it.

"Just Got Paid"

"Mushmouth Shoutin'." Pete played acoustic guitar and got credit for doing so. He was out of tune but they used the track anyway because it sounded bluesy.

"Ko Ko Blue"

"Chevrolet"

"Apologies to Pearly." Billy had played for years with a classic '59 Les Paul guitar he named Miss Pearly Gates. This time he cut the tune with a Fender Stratocaster, hence the name.

"Some Bar-B-Que." Pearly was back in hand and her unique tone is showcased here.

"Sure Got Cold After the Rain Fell." Guitar through a slow Leslie organ speaker was again used and Billy played some of the most from-the-heart and personal guitar he ever recorded.

"Whiskey 'n' Mama." Just as "Thunderbird" was originally called "C Shuffle," this one was a jam tune originally called "G 4/4."

"Down Brownie." Billy tried to play like Richards and sing like Jagger, with mixed success.

TRES HOMBRES (1973)

One of the alternative photographs of the Mexican dinner on the inner cover showed prophylactics draped all around the food. For obvious reasons it never saw the light of day.

"Waitin' for the Bus." According to Billy, when he went to buy his first Cadillac (an El Dorado) he actually took the bus to get to the car lot.

"Jesus Just Left Chicago." Don Fox, the New Orleans promoter (originally from Chicago) thinks this song is about him. It isn't. On tour, ZZ referred to the song as "Jesus Was a Chicano," which made sense to nobody (except the band).

"Beer Drinkers and Hell Raisers." It started out as a version of "Barefootin' " at a sound check in a tobacco warehouse in Kentucky. The stage that night consisted of two flatbed tobacco trucks parked side by side.

"Master of Sparks." This tune may once have been Steve Perron's. Both he and Billy claimed to have witnessed a guy strap himself into a steel sphere and get pushed out of a pickup truck at fifty miles per hour, thereby providing the inspiration for the name. At times Billy has been known to claim that he made the ride himself! At last communication on the subject, Billy says the sphere has been made into a deer blind and is somewhere in Texas.

"Hot, Blue, and Righteous." The third tune Billy played through the Leslie organ speaker. Frank and Dusty told me that Bill Ham sang a background vocal.

"Move Me On Down the Line"

"Precious and Grace." This is about two female hitchhikers—fresh out of prison and horny as bisexual minks—that Billy and Dusty picked up driving back from Dallas.

"La Grange."—Frank and Dusty told me that it was written on the way to Robin Hood Brian's studio in Tyler, Texas.

"Sheik."—The wah-wah pedal made a rare, soulful appearance.

"Have You Heard?"—ZZ Top testifies.

FANDANGO (1975)

This album was done half live and half in the studio. The live side captured one of the worst performances I ever heard ZZ play. I think Billy was nervous because he knew he was being recorded. Don Fox was the announcer, and he gave Bill Ham his word that he wouldn't cuss when he introduced the band, but he did anyway.

LIVE SIDE
"Thunderbird"
"Jailhouse Rock"
"Backdoor Medley"

STUDIO SIDE
"Nasty Dogs and Funky Kings." This was heavily influenced by Fleetwood Mac's original guitar player, Peter Green—one of Billy's favorite guitarists—on the Fleetwood Mac song "Searching for Madge."
"Blue Jean Blues." I think Billy was inspired by some woman troubles he was having at the time.
"Balinese." Nope, nobody had been to Indonesia. There once was a famous gambling club in Galveston, Texas, by this name. Billy's father gigged there in its heyday.
"Mexican Blackbird." The inspiration was a whore ZZ met who had a Black father and a Mexican mother. I have seen a picture of her that was taken with the band.
"Heard It On the X." Back when there were more restrictions on what material could be played over the airwaves—along with restrictions on how much power a station could use to send their signal—radio stations with megawatt transmitters located just over the border in Mexico provided music that was then considered controversial. ZZ Top was grateful, and offered their tribute to stations XERB and XERF.
"Tush." I think the title originated with Richard Choerne, a guest roadie we had out at one time. He was always saying, "Loogathadush!" which is mushmouth for "Look at the tush!" The band had never heard *tush* used as slang for ass until meeting Richard. According to Frank, Dusty cut the vocal with his shirt off, sweating like a pig.

TEJAS (1976)

"It's Only Love"
"Arrested for Driving While Blind." Rumor has it that Billy's once-upon-a-time friend Kurt Linhof wrote part of this.
"El Diablo." Mexican double agent Fred Carrasco had just fatally aborted his escape from the state prison in Huntsville, Texas, and is memorialized here.

"Snappy Kakkie"
"Enjoy and Get It On." Inspired by the House of Pies.
"Ten Dollar Man." The Boys met a coked-out record promotion man.
"Pan Am Highway Blues"
"Avalon Hideaway." Inspired by the Avalon Drugstore in Houston.
"She's a Heartbreaker." One of the lyrics, "flagrant fuzzy," was taken from the name of a fart (the "fragrant fuzzy") in a British novelty record entitled "The Crepitation Contest." It just goes to show that no source of inspiration is too shallow.
"Asleep in the Desert." The middle part was originally a tune Billy called "Pearly's Prayer."

THE BEST OF ZZ TOP (1977)

This album was released without the full blessings of Bill Ham, to say the least. In part because London Records "done him wrong" by not consulting him about it, Ham took ZZ Top to Warner.

"Tush"
"Waitin' for the Bus"
"Jesus Just Left Chicago"
"Francine"
"Just Got Paid"
"La Grange"
"Blue Jean Blues"
"Backdoor Love Affair"
"Beer Drinkers and Hell Raisers"
"Heard It On the X"

DEGUELLO (1979)

It took almost three years before the transition was completed from London to Warner, a long time for the Boys to sit around and contemplate their navels. There was a distinctly weird change of image during that time period for ZZ Top, from rural Texan to neo-punk.

"I Thank You." By total coincidence Bonnie Raitt released an album at about the same time ZZ released theirs, with this same Sam and Dave song on it.
"She Loves My Automobile"
"I'm Bad, I'm Nationwide"

"A Fool for Your Stockings"

"Manic Mechanic." The true manic mechanic is Claude Matte. Frank and Dusty will never forget Matte reaching up under the dash of their battered Triumph automobile and jerking out a tangle of vacuum lines and wires with the casual comment, "You don't need dese," and then asking for a hammer so he could make a "slight adjustment."

"Dust My Broom"

"Lowdown in the Street." The music scene in 1970s Austin is described.

"Hi Fi Mama"

"Cheap Sunglasses." Billy really does like cheap sunglasses.

"Esther Be the One." This one seems to be sort of a Gibbons salute to Elvis Costello.

EL LOCO (1981)

In my opinion, this has to qualify as one of the least impressive album covers ever, although it is kinda funny.

"Tube Snake Boogie"

"I Wanna Drive You Home"

"Ten Foot Pole." Some people think that the lyrics are sung with a "mush-mouth," but the truth is they don't exist. Billy always claimed that it was about the Abominable Snowman, but the jury is still out on that one.

"Leila." Mark Erlewine played the pedal steel guitar.

"Don't Tease Me"

"It's So Hard"

"Pearl Necklace." Not as innocent as it seems, this title is a double *entendre* for having oral sex performed and then ejaculating on the female's chest.

"Groovy Little Hippie Pad"

"Heaven, Hell, or Houston." This was a farcical sound-check tune that Billy made up about a wino passing out handbills in Houston. It was about ten years before he added the slide guitar part and got around to recording the song.

"Party on the Patio." The alternate name, as used on tour, was "Party in Her Pantyhose."

ELIMINATOR (1983)

This will probably be the all-time best-selling ZZ Top album. The timing, planning, and material were right on target, and the results were obvious.

"Gimmee All Your Lovin' "

"Got Me Under Pressure." Billy and Linden Hudson wrote and recorded this on a demo tape in one afternoon without Dusty or Frank around.

"Sharp Dressed Man." I argued with him that the title should be "Well Dressed Man," but Billy was adamant.

"Legs." Linden introduced the pumping synthesizer effect. He was even phoned by ZZ's studio engineer, Terry Manning, and asked to describe how he did it.

"Thug." Linden parted company with ZZ Top over this one, when his copyright was violated. The out-of-court settlement earned his side $600,000. Gibbons played the bass part instead of Dusty.

"TV Dinners." The original title was "Problems."

"Dirty Dog." The original title was "Scurvy Dog."

"If I Could Only Flag Her Down"

"Bad Girl." Billy told me that the raspy, high-ranged, straining vocal was done in a single take, because that was all he had in him.

AFTERBURNER (1985)

Since I was no longer with the band at this point my comments are minimal.

"Sleeping Bag"

"Stages"

"Woke Up with Wood." The title refers to a morning hard-on.

"Rough Boy"

"Can't Stop Rockin'." This was a throw-out tune that didn't make the *Eliminator* album.

"Planet of Women"

"I Got the Message"

"Velcro Fly"

"Dipping Low (in the Lap of Luxury)"

"Delirious." This was an acid rock flashback originally recorded as a psychedelic joke tune during the *Deguello* sessions, and reworked for this album.

RECYCLER (1990)

Five years between albums is a long time for fans to wait, but success of the tour and album demonstrated Ham's perfect pitch and timing as a music manager. Although the music harks back to roots in ZZ Top's 1970s phase, ergo the recycler theme, the hype is pure cars, girls, and beer as Ham focuses on use of the "-er" device.

"Concrete and Steel." Another obvious reference to erection.

"Love Thing"

"Penthouse Eyes"

"Tell It"

"My Head's in Mississippi." A new solid boogie tune to take over where "La Grange" left off.

"Give It Up." If any one of the Boys needed to have somebody "tell me where it's at," he might be too old to be worrying about anybody "giving it up."

"2000 Blues." I don't think Billy will ever make an album without at least one slow, smooth blues tune.

"Burger Man." Along with being humorous, the lyrics are pure sexual innuendo ZZ style, but they ought to give it to George Foreman as a theme song.

"Double Back." ZZ Top's contribution to the movie soundtrack of *Back to the Future III*, in which they debuted on the silver screen. Dusty quipped during an interview that ZZ didn't need wardrobe attention—they just appeared in their normal, around-Houston attire. Except for the pistol Dusty wore, that might be close to the truth.

THE ZZ TOP ROADIE ROSTER

The following list of those who worked behind the scenes is as complete as I can recall. Anybody omitted due to oversight or ignorance, *please* forgive me. My thanks and best wishes go out to all those people who gave a part of themselves to ZZ Top over the years. All they asked for in return was some Texas Boogie.

ORIGINAL CREW

Ricky Staffacher; Pete Tickle; Dave Blayney

REGULARS (TWO TOURS PLUS)

Randy Fletcher; J. W. Williams; Dave "Grizz" Rowe; Steve "Rod Reno" Deaver; "Bougre" Vickery; "Fast Terry" Van Vickle; Jimmy Emerson; Donny Stuart; Doug Chappell

"GUEST" ROADIES

Jay Boy Adams; Rusty Burns; Richard Choerne; Jim Austin; "Shotgun" Mike; Charlie Emerson; Randy Tickle; Dan Stuart; Don Gainey; Dan Mitchell; Scott from Ardent; Jerry Knight

SOUND COMPANY PERSONNEL

Rusty Bruche; M. L. Procise; John Blasutta; Craig Schertz; Buford Jones; Robin Magruder; Jack Maxon; J. W. Roberts; John Badenhop; Mark Hughes; Charlie Parnell; Mike Huff; Morris Lyda; E. Watson Hudgens; Al Childress; Jerry Cameron; Jerry Morris; Gary Patton; Zeke Ranucci; Rick "Crazy Mickey" Tresize; Bob Bogdanovich; Simon; "Mad John"; Bob Heil; Maurice; Skip; "The Evening Breeze"; Randy; Billy; George Wilkerson; "Rhino"

LIGHTING COMPANY PERSONNEL

Bobby Gorden; Brian Marshall; Jim Coatney; Chris "The Bullet"; Ben Wilson; Jerry Julian; The TERI Twins; Bob See; Tony Mazzuchi; "Handsome John"; Bill McManus; John Roth; Phil; Tom Littrell; Larry Sizemore; Gary Carnes; Jim Moody; Tina; John Blackman; Russel "Bits" Lyons; "Terp"; Phil Seaman; Dale Polansky; Eric; Ed Wannabo; Felicia; Dirk Arnold; Robert Gersh; Mac Mosier; Mark Griffin; Mick; Peter and Gorden Barden; Mike Abdosh; Greg Painter; Bill Thompson; Allan Branton

LASERS

Steve Jander; Hergie; "English" John; and a brief but memorable appearance by "Wiggy"

TRUCKERS

Joe DeAnda; Mert Mead; "Jamie Beef"; Joe Allbright; Pete DeAnda; Jo Jo Muscanare; Tom "Punchline" Duncan; "Crazy John" Weathered; John Ininguez; Paul Boren; "Sweet William"; "Turnpike Mike"; "Koko"; Jay "Commodore" Wheatley; Phillip

BUSSERS

Gerald Howell; W. C. Dunlap; Larry Dunlap; Sammy Ammons; "Hollywood Bob"; Tommy Pearson

RIGGERS

Tony Kirkpatrick; "Moose" Clemmer; "Jack the Rigger"; Dean Hart

GOOD OL' BOYS

Jim Osborn; Gene Mayer; Jim Lander; "Bullet Bob"; "Coach" South; Buddy Howell; Danny Eaton; George Maxey; Shawn Hoover; Bill Narum; "Killer Gene"; Gary Zumwalt; John Sousi; Tommy Bellhowsen; Dale "Breaux" Reed; "Caddyshack" Jay; Steve Moore; Mark Lee; Larry "Big Tool" Gorley; Clayton Faught; Donald Petifil; Paul Seward

HOT OL' GALS

Linda Andrews; Sig McKenna; Sue Emil; Meg; Brenda; Melissa Dumas; Debbie Andrews; Katy; Jana South; Linda Lesser

INDEX